This publication contains the opinions and ideas of its author. It is intended to provide helpful and informative material on the subjects addressed in the publication. It is sold with the understanding that the author and publisher are not engaged in rendering accounting, financial or investment advice or any other kind of personal professional services in the book. The reader should consult their accountancy, legal and other competent professionals before adopting any of the suggestions in this book or drawing inferences from it.

The author and publisher specifically disclaim all responsibility for any liability, loss, or risk, personal or otherwise, which is incurred as a consequence, directly or indirectly, of the use and application of any of the contents of this book.

ISBN- 10: 0-9850027- 1

ISBN- 13: 978-0-9850027 -5-6

Excerpts from the Book

- Rent Roll Triangle (RRT) is a calculation. RRT is a grading system to allow buyers to determine strength of income based on interactive variables.

- This book is a do-it-yourself version of the incredible analytical financial processing power that you can perform on your own with the app, simple pen and paper or a single page spreadsheet.

- What if you could grade any rental property- anytime- anywhere in three easy steps? How much time would that save you?

- For owners of real estate assets RRT allows you to quickly review operational outcomes and compare and contrast your assets to similar assets in the marketplace.

- RRT is your road map providing clear outcomes about where an asset stands in real time.

- For the professional investor the advantage of deploying RRT is time saved during the due diligence phase.

- The variables in the RRT calculation are the "keys to the kingdom" in terms of determining quality and strength of income for a rental property.

- For people that invest in real estate assets passively as part of their investment portfolio RRT is a tool to review and rate assets and property management based on performance.

- The outputs from RRT represent an insightful perspective about the current operations of an asset operated as a rental property.

- For property managers RRT allows you to gain more business by presenting to potential clients your in-depth knowledge of the market, the asset and how to make improvements to operations under your management.

- The sustainability and success of a rental property is based on collections.

- There is a direct correlation between the number of tenants that remain in-place for an extended period and the profitability of rental property.

- This is a specialty book for people involved in the acquisition and property management of rental property. USE WITH CAUTION.

- Use of the Rent Roll Triangle points you in the direction of action steps to improve financial operations, however, doing so to the exclusion of all else is folly…

- RRT (%) does provide an indication of how well one property might perform as opposed to another.

About the Author:

This book by John Wilhoit represents an industry standard on how to take rental revenue analysis to the next level. With this simple-to-use tool, you can get to the "first cut" without computing power and hours and hours of analysis. Of course, a serious investor will follow with deep due diligence to validate any initial outputs.

John Wilhoit has a Bachelor of Science in Business Management and a graduate degree in Urban Planning. In this book, John takes you through Rent Roll Triangle systematically. John's approach to rental property analysis is rooted in his 20+ years of experience in asset management and the property management profession.

His perspective is further broadened by experience in the public sector for federal and state agencies and in asset management for a publically-traded real estate investment trust. As an asset manager and owner–operator of apartments, condominiums and townhomes, John has developed his approach by administrating thousands of apartments across the United States from pre-construction through development and lease-up and stabilized operations.

This book is a do-it-yourself version of incredible analytical financial processing power that you can perform on your own with the app, simple pen and paper or a single page spreadsheet. This book will assist investors, owners and managers of rental property in reaching their real estate goals by using Rent Roll Triangle to distinguish strengths and weaknesses at-a-glance allowing more time during due diligence to focus on those areas that impact financial outcomes.

Wouldn't it be great to separate performance of the 90th percentile from the 40th percentile in the first twenty minutes? The ever-true odd thing about this is that in too many instances the price of both deals is about the same!

His blog, Multifamily Insight, provides John's perspective on the world of multifamily acquisitions, management and investing. To subscribe, go to www.multifamilyinsight.net.

John is the author of *How To Read A Rent Roll: A Guide to Understanding Rental Income and Multifamily Insight Volume I, II and III; How to build wealth through buying the right multifamily assets in the right markets.*
You will love John's books and the industry expertise and insight that he shares.

Join the conversation at <u>JohnWilhoit.com</u> for updates, blogs, books and podcast.

Preface:

What if you could grade any rental property, anytime, anywhere in three easy steps? How much time would that save you? Like a standardized test, results from applying the concepts found within this book will clearly present rental property income strengths and weaknesses. This is the first step to furthering your knowledge and making improvements to enhance value. Calculating a "snapshot" score using the Rent Roll Triangle formula provides you- the real estate owner, investor, lender, service provider, appraiser, manager- with an immediate starting point with guidance on where to focus your attention to affect improvements in cash flow.

Rent Roll Triangle™ (RRT) emphasizes the powerful interaction between three property specific variables; current rents, or stated rents (from the lease), collected rents (actual collections), and the term of in–place leases (lease term) in predicting strength of income. The outcome produces a grade from 0 to 100%. The higher the percentage, the higher the strength of income.

RRT represents a type of sensitivity analysis that anyone can use to assess rental property income. Yes, it's great to have super-computer processing power to grind data into packets the size of sand, yet for everyday use, most people want a solution they can scratch on a single piece of paper or pound out in minutes on a single spreadsheet. RRT offers that solution.

A lease and the lease term represent rental revenue. Each lease reflects an anticipated amount of income for a set amount of time in exchange for the property owner providing the property in a usable condition to meet the uses described in the lease. The value of any income producing asset is based on the value attributed to the leases. *The money is in the leases.*

In commercial real estate, analysts devote a significant amount of time to "sensitivity analysis." This is code for attempting to determine what will occur next...next month, next quarter and next year. Another form of sensitivity analysis is factoring in cause and effect; if A occurs what happens to B?

In my book, <u>How To Read A Rent Roll</u> I provided the premise for RRT. This book focuses exclusively on the use of RRT as a functional tool in rental income sensitivity analysis providing case studies with various real estate asset types. This book outlines the statistical and empirical data to support the hypothesis of RRT in anticipation that it will becomes part of your real estate decision-making tool box.

Table of Contents

Introduction

A real estate asset manager, a scientist and a zoologist walk into a bar. The asset manager (that would be me) knows real estate operations and metrics, the scientist knows mathematics and statistics, the zoologist studies patterns in wildlife, many of which are applicable to how investment criteria are formed. The asset manager doodles on the back of a napkin a premise for measuring income elasticity in rental income. The scientist takes the crude math and creates a calculation. The zoologist forms an opinion about how the formula will affect various species (different property types). Rent Roll Triangle (RRT) is born. It's good to have a team!

Discovering the strengths and weaknesses in asset operations with RRT guides you to focus on those areas of operations that most impact revenue and therefore most impact value. Real estate investing is all about compartmentalizing risk. The better you are at this the better your investment decisions. Few people invest their money without a presumed yield in mind. The Rent Roll Triangle™ (RRT) assists in compartmentalizing strengths and weaknesses in rental revenue and identifying areas of concern pre-acquisition. It is an evidence based approach.

The three property specific variables that make up the triangle are:

- Stated Lease Rent (SLR – stated rents per in–force leases)
- Collected Rent (CR – actual collections)
- Lease Term (LT – percent of lease term fulfilled)

A rent roll is the focal point of determining value. That is what makes rent roll analysis so important. To "grade" the quality of rental income allows for focusing due diligence efforts on properties under consideration that have the greatest potential given your risk tolerance and yield requirements. Although there are four variables used in the formula, the triangle namesake of this book includes the three variables that are property specific; thus, the triangle. The fourth measure, Gross Potential Rent, is a market–wide measure.

The outcome obtained from RRT is a percentage of maximum rental income the asset can generate. Therefore, the higher the percentage the closer the asset is to operating at its maximum financial potential. The Rent Roll Triangle (RRT) is a measure of rental income stability. It captures the relationship between stated lease rents (SLR), collected rents (CR), and the lease term (LT), and measures performance on a percentage scale from zero to one hundred with one hundred being perfected financial outputs for the asset in question. Although there are four variables we refer to this as a triangle because three of the measures are property specific. Gross Potential Rent is a market–wide measure.

This is a specialty book for people involved in the acquisition and property management of rental property. USE WITH CAUTION. Mastery of the concepts will make you feel as if you have superior knowledge and the ability to time the market. I have never met anyone that can successfully time the market- any market (the exception being Sam Zell, former President of Equity Trust- who has not so much timed the market but knew how to profitably exploit market opportunities). Use of the Rent Roll Triangle (RRT) is not a market timing devise; it is a revenue sensitivity tool to assist you in determining areas of strength and weakness from income producing real property assets.

Use of the Rent Roll Triangle points you in the direction of action steps to improve financial operations, however, doing so to the exclusion of all else is folly without an over-arching plan that accounts for other operational aspects.

People with superior knowledge and limited experience make mistakes. So, take your time with implementation of the techniques discussed herein until you understand how the concepts influence your perception of value. Here is a simple example.

A newly purchased four-building asset is in dire need of new roofs, windows and paint. An inexperienced operator starts painting everything immediately thinking this is the least expensive method to increase value. An experienced operator completes all repairs to a single building first, then moves to the next building. The experienced operator understands that having all repairs accomplished to a single building will produce higher rents for that building. Note that these "buildings" could represent four units in each building or forty units in each building. The concept remains the same.

Knowledge is power and power brings change. Prior to changing "everything" based on new knowledge slow down a little. Breathe. Contemplate. Draw up a plan of action- then implement; measure twice and cut once. This is so simple, yet so powerful.

Specialized knowledge, like that represented with Rent Roll Triangle, can cause good or evil. Said another way; do not hurt yourself with this new, sharp razor of action steps (see prior paragraph).

RRT lays out strengths and weaknesses of a rental property asset utilizing the selected variables; however, there are "always" more variables than those presented in the control group. Thus, whereas with RRT you can shine a bright light on the variables we discuss in detail, try to avoid a myopic perspective that excludes other potential pitfalls.

Every pilot has a flight checklist they utilize prior to departure of each flight. Consider RRT as part of you pre-flight, pre-acquisition checklist for rental property acquisitions. With pilot's it doesn't matter the length of the flight- they use their checklist. With RRT it doesn't matter the size of the deal…the checklist remains an important part of the pre-acquisition asset review.

As a real estate investor, you anticipate a certain cash flow (outcome) from invested dollars. It is one thing to pay a premium for a high level of predictability, the worst outcome is over-paying for a low level of predictability. Applying an initial grade, a first cut financial looksee, to an asset can assist you in determining where to focus your time and attention. Better to focus on those assets with the highest capacity of delivering a predictable yield and leave the rest in the dust. Quickly.

As an owner of rental property, utilize RRT to measure your operations against potential maximum financial outputs that a rental property asset can generate. RRT will assist you in measuring present day operations against potential gains in revenue. This book will assist you in identifying and isolating operational areas to improve. The financial condition of your assets should improve incrementally from the knowledge you gain as you focus on the individual aspects of the RRT formula. You will learn the pressure points that require your attention. These will usually be the same pressure points that generate increases in cash flow, and in turn, increases in the underlying value of the assets.

Each case study provides a little different look at RRT as the formula scores rental property assets related to strength of income. Thus, while every case study is unique, the quantifiable outcomes delivered by RRT are normalized to reflect a static number from the inputs utilized for each case.

What makes this so important? First, you can perform this analysis yourself; no high-powered computer resources, MBA's or calculus required. Second, this scoring system can become "part" of your due diligence process as a baseline for comparison of comparable assets under consideration. Capitalization rates are fine, knowing the internal rate of return and cash flow is all part of getting to know the financial capacity of an asset. RRT is that one more layer: looking at and under the numbers and identifying strengths and weaknesses to address, improve or eliminate.

Also, RRT is a tool to use in negotiations with sellers. While you may or may not decide to share your scoring system based on the outcomes derived from RRT, you can express (in plain English) why you believe an offer of X is a good offer and back up your statements with definitive expressions identified from your research and financial review of the subject asset.

Add to this that once you have mastered RRT the formula can potentially shorten your due diligence time and money spent by rapidly excluding certain assets under consideration. Considering your "buyers box" those assets falling outside of your parameters (as determined by you and assisted by RRT) requires no further consideration allowing for re-direction of your efforts to assets with greater potential.

The Case study format in Part V presents various types of rental property interacting with the formula. Every investor has a different set of eyes. Depending on how you intend to use RRT, consider each case as a potential acquisition candidate, an owned asset, for reviewing comparable assets or as an asset manager or property manager.

Part 1

Rent Roll Triangle (RRT)

What is the Rent Roll Triangle?

Rent Roll Triangle (RRT) is a calculation. RRT is a grading system to determine strength of income based on interactive variables. As an evidence based approach, RRT is inherently about rental revenue. RRT excludes factors related to the age of a property, its condition or location. RRT is a starting point to identify further actions necessary to remedy gaps in revenue between Gross Potential Rent, Stated Lease Rent and Collected Rent.

 For the professional real estate investor, for companies with fully staffed due diligence departments and for the full-time investment advisors with server based financial algorithms at their fingertips, the prior paragraph doesn't mean much. Sure, they can add RRT as another layer to they're fully built investment decision-making systems. RRT will have significantly greater impact for investors outside of the realm of those mentioned above.

RRT can be calculated with pen and paper in the five-dollar calculator. It will assist the doctor looking to purchase the Medical office building. It will be of great benefit to the young couple looking to acquire their first commercial real estate asset. It will help the small investor (on deals under $10,000,000) to secure an independent thought process outside of the document box with 500 pages of information with no conclusions about financial validity, rationale or usefulness within those pages.

In Frank Gallinelli's book *What Every Investor Needs to Know About Cash Flow*, you will find a multitude of calculations that are tried and true. What is represented with RRT is just a slightly different view through the prism of real estate investment analysis and due diligence. It doesn't bend the numbers nor attempt to take you astray. It simply asking you to seek and find relevant rental income information and apply it to the property as an apples to apples and oranges to oranges comparison of operational outcomes. Is this a difficult task? It does require earnest research. It does require validating the numbers used the calculation. Tying off the numbers in this way should add a small amount of additional comfort in the due diligence process deployed by both full-time professionals, individuals and family purchasing rental property assets.

Analogous to "Iron Triangle," a term used by political scientists to describe the strong ties between Congress, Bureaucracy, and Interest Groups in the United States in matters of policy, the RRT emphasizes the powerful interaction of gross potential rents, current, or stated rents (from the lease), collected rents (collections), and the term of in–place leases (lease terms) in predicting strength of income. The outcome produces a grade – 0 to 100%. The higher the grade, the higher the strength of income.

Before starting a road trip, the first step is to know where you are on the map. The Rent Roll Triangle™ (RRT) furnishes pinpoint accuracy as to where a rental property is in terms of financial performance and identifies very quickly the areas of concern. With this information, you can focus your attention on remedies that will have the greatest impact on strengthening the financial performance of the asset.

Rent Roll Triangle (RRT) represents a type of sensitivity analysis that anyone can use to assess rental property income. Yes, it's great to have super-computer processing power to grind data into packets the size of sand, yet for everyday use, most people want a solution they can scratch on a single piece of paper or pound out in minutes on a single spreadsheet. RRT offers that solution.

RRT identifies strengths and weakness in rental property revenue. Once known, you can implement fixes to remedy problems and push positive financial outputs. It is not enough to know the areas of concern and leave them untouched. Is an un-cashed check money? Not until it clears, right? The same holds true with RRT; find the money, get the money, put it in the bank. Where is the money? It's in the leases.

A lease and the lease term represent the legal right to collect rental revenue of a certain amount for a certain length of time. Each lease reflects an anticipated amount of income for a set amount of time in exchange for the property owner providing the property in a usable condition to meet the uses described in the lease. The value of any income-producing asset stands in large part on the value attributed to the leases. The money is in the leases.

In commercial real estate, analysts devote a significant amount of time to "sensitivity analysis". This is code for attempting to determine what will happen next...next month, next quarter and next year. Another form of sensitivity analysis is to determine cause and effect. If A occurs what happens to B?

RRT is your road map providing clear outcomes about where an asset stands in real time. It is not, however, a substitute for contemporary forms of financial analysis; it does not take the place of reviewing financials, service and utility invoices or property tax returns. Performing the RRT calculation for each asset in your portfolio generates specific data points as a springboard to next steps: no running in the dark with scissors or guessing where to find financial weaknesses.

Most income property is acquired for long-term ownership; five-years, ten-years, twenty-years, etc. Thus, while it is important to know the current income, it is equally if not more important to understand the viability of the asset and its income stream going forward.

Rent Roll Triangle™ (RRT) is a simple calculation to measure the stability of rental income based on gross potential rent, stated lease rents, collections and lease term.

The higher the percentage the closer the asset is to operating at its maximum financial potential. Rent Roll Triangle™ (RRT) is a measure of rental income stability. It captures the relationship between stated lease rents (SLR), collected rents (CR), and the lease term (LT), measuring performance on a percentage scale from zero to one hundred with one hundred being perfected financial output- maximum revenue.

Although there are four variables, I refer to this as a triangle because three of the measures are property specific. Gross Potential Rent (GPR) is a market–wide measure. GPR is that carrot that keeps the horse moving forward. Seldom does it remain constant as you and competitors in your marketplace attempt to push rents up. Granted, it is a two-edged sword as economic paradigms shift and changes to the competitive marketplace can place downward pressure on GPR.

The outcome from RRT is the current percentage of maximum rental income the asset can generate as compared to Gross Potential Rent considering the term of the lease.

Rent Roll Triangle™ (RRT) solves the problem of estimating relative stability of income for a rental property. Further scholarly research of RRT, I anticipate, will point to a greater understanding of the relationship between the variables.

With respect to rental income, RRT immediately points to actionable areas of concern.

Components of the Rent Roll Triangle (RRT) are: gross potential rents (GPR), stated lease rents (SLR rent per the terms of in–force lease), collected rents (CR) and term of tenancy (lease term or LT). The individual elements of RRT represent the four variables within the equation. A significant change in any one variable changes the outcome of the calculation and conveys to ownership and management where to focus time and attention to remedy. Big gap between GPR and SL? Find out why and remedy. Big gap between SL and CR? Review credit quality. Short LT? Why and for how long- what is the cause. Find out why and remedy. RRT assist in finding solutions faster by knowing where to look.

RRT localizes rent income problems allowing operators to address the area of concern in real time.

Reaching the number generated by RRT will create more questions. These questions provide further insight about the stability, or quality, of rental income from the application of RRT to rental property. RRT is simply one more method of viewing an income–producing asset. Relying on any single number to determine value is shortsighted. Use caution against overreliance on any one measure including RRT.

The upfront work is in obtaining actual data for use in the equation. As they say, garbage in, garbage out, so the numbers collected for solving RRT must be accurate.

With respect to rental income, RRT points to actionable areas of concern. RRT localizes rental income problems allowing you to identify issues in real time. How? By interlocking the four variables and highlighting the disparities between them. For example:

- By identifying a significant gap between Gross Potential Rent (GPR) and stated lease rents (SLR). If SLR is far below GPR one question to ask is if this differential is market–wide or property specific? If market–wide, then this knowledge allows you to form competitive concessions to compete more effectively.

- If SLR (actual rents per the lease) are well below GPR, then the issue might be simple mismanagement. Perhaps current management or ownership doesn't care. Perhaps rents are low because the property cannot effectively compete due to its current physical condition.

- Assuming collections (Collected Rent) are an issue, you know this is directly linked to resident underwriting.

- Identification of leases where residents are departing prior to their lease term expiring. This problem could relate to resident screening or how management handles maintenance. The problem could be that management has dozens of unanswered maintenance calls. Or, the issue could be a wildly competitive market with neighboring properties cannibalizing each other just to capture any incremental occupancy increases.

On the revenue side, narrowing the discussion to factors that most affect rental income allows you to cut to the problem area early in your review and see what's under the hood. Will the patient respond to treatment? Do you have the right team to administer treatment given your yield requirements and expertise? Do you want to perform this treatment or move on to another property with greater profit potential?

RRT is a starting point to identify further actions necessary to remedy gaps in revenue between GPR, SLR and CR. RRT does not consider physical property attributes, age, deferred maintenance, traffic counts or new competition entering the marketplace. While these are of consideration by the serious investor, the calculation is void of any representation about such. At the same time, a lower score versus a higher score will invariably tie back into the condition of the asset and its apparent competition within the market are where the asset competes.

Many assets will be shooting towards attaining a higher RRT score from a current operational stanza that will benefit from professional property management and implementing actions that drive revenue. For assets with scores nearing 100% the RRT representation is that the asset is near maximum revenue potential as the asset is presently operated. Changes to operational strategy, which in turn changes GPR, requires a new RRT calculation taking into consideration the new operational persona. A warehouse turned nightclub, a parking lot turned weekend market, a regional mall shuttering its food court for five specialty hi-end restaurants and bars… have all reset GPR for the asset.

RRT Simplified

While I hesitate to trade speed for accuracy, this is part of daily life and investment decision-making life. It is presented here as a shortcut to the long version RRT equation, but not recommended as a substitute for the long version equation. However, expediency has its place, therefore, to gain a speedy RRT calculation, do the following:

Divide Collected Rents by Gross Potential Rent and multiply the outcome by Lease Term percent

Now that the nuts and bolts and (sometimes) pretzel-like processes are behind us, let's simplify. There are many people with the unenviable task of sorting through a never-ending deal flow. They are often in a damned if they do, damned if they don't position, whereas their job is to assess potential acquisitions and bring to fore those with the best possible opportunity to profit. And there are so many! And most are just plain junk (for the buyer).

Deals and deal flow outside of an investors focal point are just noise for a buyer because if the investor specialty is medical office it doesn't matter how many raw land deals come across their desk - they are of no consequence. To the buyer, for example, potential acquisitions (or deals) can be junk if the investor specialty is warehouse in the southeast there is no need to review hotels in the northwest. Setting aside the obvious, even with known property type and geography set in stone there is often a level of deal flow that exceeds staff ability to review each deal in detail. Enter RRT Simplified.

Consider running each deal that fits your property type and geographic criteria through RRT Simplified as an initial first step. Those that show promise go to the head of the line for further consideration.

Mathematically, there is a simplified version of the RRT (%), in which SLR is removed from the formula, as below:

Simplified:

RRT (%) = ((CR / GPR)(LT/12])/12) X 100)

With the following example, this shortened form is as follows:

Gross Potential Rent: GPR = $3,300,000

Collected Rents: CR = $2,950,000

Lease Term: LT = 12 months'

RRT (%) = (($2,950,000/$3,300,000)((12 - [12-12])/12) X 100)

= 89.39 %

Simplified further...

Divide Collected Rents by Gross Potential Rent and multiply the outcome by Lease Term percent

This simplified version takes the original RRT (%) formula and rearranged two factors. First, we kept the Stated Lease Rents (SLR) as the numerator of the first factor, but moved (or exchanged) the denominators between the first and second factors. These rearrangements are allowable with multiplication of fractions, and their correctness can be demonstrated with mathematical proofs. The simplified version follows perfectly legal mathematical rules. The rearrangement is shown below:

Original RRT (%) = ((SLR / GPR)(CR/SLR)((LT/12])/12)) X 100),

can be rearranged

RRT (%) = ((SLR/SLR)(CR/GPR)((LT/12])/12)) X 100).

Then, the SLR as both the numerator and the denominator as the first factor "cancel out" (much as 4/4 is equal to one; or, 15/15 is equal to one; or, more generally, a/a is equal to one), leaving the first factor equal to "1"

so, the equation simplifies to

RRT (%) = ((CR / GPR)(LT/12])/12) X 100),

the one used in the example above.

One practical interpretation of this mathematical simplification is that knowing the actual Stated Lease Rents is unnecessary for the calculation of RRT (%), because it contributes with equal strength to the numerator of the first factor as it contributes to the denominator of the second term. This is useful to know if, for example, you are unable to obtain high quality information about Stated Lease Rents, or if you believe the information obtained is unreliable. We prefer to keep Stated Lease Rents in the overall equation, however, partly because it remains an important stand-alone consideration in deciding whether to invest in a potential real estate asset.

How to Make Money with RRT

Discovering the strengths and weaknesses in asset operations with RRT guides you to focus on those areas that most impact revenue and therefore most impact value while getting to conclusions faster and saving a ton of time. Having the "real" numbers is imperative when deploying this evidence-based calculation. In the fast-paced world of rental property due diligence there is often a lag between the time a seller delivers glossy proforma's and real operational numbers. It's up to you to keep these data sets segregated never confusing one for the other.

As a pre-acquisition, due diligence tool. Time is money and there are times when there are more deals that seconds in a minute. How do you cut the clutter- fast? Use the RRT % to find out in sixty seconds where the deal stands as compared to competing assets. Use the calculation to compare competitive assets and identify what is most affecting current income. Then focus your attention on asset showing most promise. Granted, promise means different things to different investors. Some are value investors seeking a bargain. The bargain investor is willing to do whatever it takes to improve valuation. For some investors, nothing is more imperative than capital preservation- they are seeking a long history of stable income with the pretense that same income stream is what they are buying into the future- as is with nominal changes required.

As an operational due diligence tool, troubleshooting pre-acquisition and outlining a plan of action ready for implementation on the day of closing is a huge time-saver. Having a fast and factual RRT score is a godsend in directing your efforts in the right direction for creating improvements that affect value and value creation. Having at your fingertips the percent disparity between GPR, SL and CR will represent the baseline information for making positive changes quickly

As a tool in negotiations. Decide if you wish to share your findings with a property seller as part of a negotiating strategy. Some buyers prefer to present a purchase price number and that's it. Some will provide an offer and bank letter to bolster their position as financially qualified to make the purchase. A buyer may share, for example, that he or she is aware that current rents are far below market rents and for this reason your offer is

11

X dollars. Many sellers of apartment properties believe reflecting a rent roll were SL is equal to CR makes for a positive presentation. The fact is when this occurs it is merely a reflection that rents are substantially below market levels. The reason that collections are at 100% is because the tenant base is aware that living anywhere in a location similar quality cost significantly more.

For the Professional investor, the advantage of deploying RRT is time saved during the due diligence phase. Due diligence time lines continue to shrink- the atypical 60-90 days is no more as 'all cash" deals are in play and committed earnest money "goes hard" in as short as hours and not days. There is simply no time to slowly rummage through the reams of data in a complicated deal without a quality system. RRT can be part of that system in terms of identifying strength of income in short order and allowing your team to focus on solutions to identified weaknesses requiring a remedy at the property level. Considering the issues found you were due diligence should tell you what attributes to look at when hiring a professional property management. Some property management firms I known for their leasing, others as no-nonsense operators. You're looking to find a fit between the property and property management firm hired that will allow asset to shine.

Also, for the professional investor, RRT can assist in culling your deal flow in this way; when reviewing deals offered at market value with a high RRT, you know very quickly there is not much value creation to pursue. Unless the asset has some strategic value, you can quickly place it in the "No" file and move on to other more lucrative potential targeted assets. The prior statement is invalid if the deal is a land play for assemblage or something with similar intriguing features.

Let's remember that "everyone" is not strictly a value investor. Paying full value for an asset that presently has a high RRT could confirm the current asking price as within reason. Some investors are willing to pay market value for an asset that meets or exceeds their investment criterion without the asset having to be a bargain. It could be in the same zip code as the owner's other investments or within a market with a trusted partner or management company. All investment decisions are not about the investment in question.

Some investors only invest in their home market; doesn't matter that yields are three percentage points higher a short flight away. Some investors are strategic, whereas, the investment allows for consolidated operations of their businesses, or creates a synergy of some sort that is non-financial to the outside observer.

An owner/operator of multifamily, for example, may be looking to only own assets in two or three contiguous zip codes because management can handle a higher volume of property without expanding staff. This represents a situation where long-term cost savings more than make up for paying full value for a single asset because the aggregate operating cost are decreased for the owned portfolio.

For owners of real estate assets, RRT allows you to quickly review operational outcomes and compare your assets to similar assets in the marketplace. Are your assets performing well against peers? What can management due to improve operations and value? When applied to owned assets, you can drill directly into an area of concern and direct staff to make that area the highest priority.

When you get to the case studies take note that each and every case can be viewed from an owner's perspective. As owners, we hope and pray that property management is engaged and has our best interest at heart. Yet as an owner there really is no such thing as passive ownership. Someone still has to watch the store and someone still should watch the good people selected to run the store.

For people that invest in real estate assets passively as part of their investment portfolio, RRT is a tool to review and rate assets based on performance. RRT can assist in selecting investment management and property management just by bringing the right questions to a meeting. Can team members responsible for operation answer basic questions; do they know GPR, SLR versus CR and LT? If the answer is no…that's a problem for you if it's your asset.

13

For property managers RRT allows you to gain more business by presenting to potential clients your in-depth knowledge of the market, the asset, and how to make improvements to operations under your management. RRT can be part of every client presentation you make going forward. As a property manager having applied RRT to a potential client's asset(s), determine if the challenge is something you can do and set your fees accordingly to provide the level of attention necessary to address asset deficiencies to retain clients for the long-term with long-term fee income. This is no "pipe dream". The ideas presented here are actionable and provide you with an opportunity to convert new business.

Market Analysis of Comparative Assets

While RRT represents a form of "sensitivity analysis" for rental property, it also allows for comparisons amongst and between similar properties. There're two types of comparative assets reviews: one is a comparison of acquisition candidates, the other is a comparison of competitive assets that compete with owned assets or potential acquisition candidates.

There are five deals on your desk all which meet your basic investment criteria what do you look for to differentiate the assets? It can be any number of things: from condition to age, upside potential to being in the path of development. From capitalization rates to NOI calculations at some point all property can begin to look like a blur from time to time. It is up to you to find points of differentiation that separates the future potential value of these assets and to do so in real-time. When comparing assets that compete with owned property or an acquisition candidate, it is your job to appropriately select competitive assets, those that compete head-to-head again your owned assets or the acquisition candidates under consideration.

Example #1. There is a low-rise office property for sale in a well-established office park. While there is uniformity in architecture lease rates vary widely as does term of tenancy. The seller states that "everyone" pays $15 a square foot in the office park. As a potential buyer, taking this information at face value would still lead to different valuations based on term of tenancy. RRT will tease out these differences as the equation is applied to different buildings within this development.

Example #2. An atypical financial review of two side-by side multifamily assets will likely reflect a higher valuation for the asset with higher stated lease rents (SLR). However, use of RRT that considers collected rents may turn the table and provide a higher score to the asset with lower stated rents and higher collections (actual cash in bank collections). In other words, the asset with lower rents may be a better buy because of higher quality residents.

Example #3. Consider two similar properties that are three-miles apart. They are alike in every way; age, condition, street visibility, parking availability, sound management and lease terms. Using RRT, you

15

determine that one property is leasing for a dollar amount vastly under Gross Potential Rents while the other is near the top of market rents. Both are being offered to the market at the same price point. RRT makes the buyer aware of the market rents differential, and could be a critical piece of information for making a quality decision between the two assets.

Part 2
Rental Property

What is Rental Property?

Rental property can be any tangible or intellectual property where the owner allows use of the property for a period in exchange for remuneration (payment). We rent many different things, however, a conversation about rent often refers to real estate property.

Saying a piece of property is perfect is like saying you have seen the perfect fastball. Even if this were true, how do you repeat it? By using a financial model, one that levels the playing field, the investor/manager/owner can implement financial analysis tool that cut through the clutter.

With ownership of rental property, the owner has certain rights to the income obtained. Without ownership of rental property, you have no rights to the income from the property. Granted, this is over-simplified, as there are a thousand legal documents to segregate rights, ownership, percentage interest, etc. We will leave this level of dissection to the legal profession.

For purposes of this writing the presumption is that there is a direct line of ownership between the property "owner" with the assumption that this person (or entity) has rights to income derived from property owned. Once the right to rents is established, with the owner or owners' representative, a potential tenant (a resident, lessor or business) can enter discussions for use of the property.

Residential property is leased to people for residential use for a flat amount for a specified time. Retail building owners rent "store fronts" to businesses for rent that is often a percentage of revenue. Some businesses rent warehouses to hold and then distribute their goods. Tech companies lease buildings for servers. Farmers rent space inside a grain silo to store their crops. Fast food restaurants rent land to build their stores. These are all examples of rental property.

Rental property is real estate property owned by one person and made available to another person for an exchange of value.

This "exchange of value" is set to a calendar. Every exchange requires a timeline (a calendar) to preserve the exchange with a beginning and end date. Owners of rental property accept money for the use of a space for a set length of time. Most residential property rents in one-year increments with payment of rent due once each month. Commercial, retail and office space leases have one, three, five and twenty year increments. Hotels rent rooms for one night at a time. These are all forms of rental property.

Having established the rights to rent, a timeline for the rental and the amount exchanged for the term, the parties set their agreement in writing, usually, with a lease document that provides certain rights to the lessee and lessor.

What is Rental Income?

Rental income is the contractual payment of rent received by owners of rental property from those that use the property for a specified purpose. In the case of rental property, the service provided is use of a dwelling or space for a period for a payment of money. Per the IRS, rental income is:

Rental income is any payment received for the use or occupation of property.

Free rent never works; someone must pay for the use of property. If usage were free, there is still a cost, namely; taxes and insurance. Therefore, there is still a cost. When rental property is leased and the lease amount is not paid the lessor (property owner) is subsidizing the lessee (tenant, or renter) by maintaining the taxes and insurance payments even though they are not receiving compensation. This is not sustainable.

Lease payments (rent) play an important part in every economy. Real estate taxes are often a large part of local governmental budgets. Owners of rental property pay real estate taxes from rent receipts. Asking non-paying tenants to move to make room for paying tenants is part of being in the rental business. It is a necessary part of assuring that rental property owners derive a return on their investment.

Contractual rental income is the single largest component of revenue from rental property.

Contractual rental income is the lifeblood of property ownership. Contractual rental income is the source of revenue that allows a property owner to operate and profit from running the business of rental property ownership. Non–paying tenants must vacate so that the owner may rent to a paying customer. Much of property law is written to allow a property owner to enforce their rights as owner. Collection of rents is a basic right of any property owner; however, a written lease remains the cornerstone of asserting owner rights.

What is a Rent Roll?

The rent roll is a snapshot of current rental income as represented by the owner of a real property asset. The rent roll is a synopsis of rent from executed leases. The rent roll is a tool to validate asset value and stability. A rent roll states the name of the payer, the address, the lease amount and the start and end date of the obligation to pay rent.

The rent roll is the property owner's representation of rental income derived from an income–producing real estate asset.

The rent roll is the controlling document for producing information to owners about the status of rents: collected rents, outstanding rents, loss-to-rents, occupancy and vacancy. It is the centerpiece of financial management. This same information is of interest to the property owner's bankers, potential buyers, insurance providers and appraisers. While they all have slightly different uses for the information they are attempting to do the same thing: determine value.

The banker is looking at lendable value. A potential buyer is reviewing the rent roll income from many different facets (see my book How To Read A Rent Roll). An insurance providers wants to determine market value and replacement value. An appraiser reviews an asset as compared to similar assets in the marketplace.

When purchasing a rental property, the rent roll and lease file review triangulate rental income validity. A review of each lease file is imperative to validating contractual rental income as reflected on the rent roll. For commercial asset's this is referred to as a Lease Abstract.

Any number represented on the rent roll must tie to the numbers and date within valid in-place leases on file. The rent roll states the lease amounts (rents). A review of valid in-place leases confirms these amounts (of rent).

A rent roll only applies to assets that generate rental income. Over-stating the obvious, properties that have value but no rental income, such as: some raw land, some public buildings, parks and trails, single-family homes that are owner occupied, there is no useful purpose for applying a rent roll to these assets.

Answers Found

I have a story to tell. I had a problem I couldn't solve. As the owner of small apartment properties (multiple assets under one hundred units) turnover was crazy high. It was eating money and creating havoc. I couldn't figure it out. My problem-solving hat said create a spreadsheet from the rent roll and look for variances asking a simple question: why are people leaving? Granted, a smarter response was to have management ask people why they were leaving. I wasn't that bright at the time so the spreadsheet was my scratchpad.

From the rent roll I created a simple spreadsheet with numbers specific to each unit: Gross Potential Rent, Stated Lease Rent, Collected Rent, rent per square foot, actual term of tenancy, average term of tenancy. The findings were pretty unimpressive; people that stayed in place longer offered greater profit potential than those that did not. Well, yea. So what? And there it was- how do you respond to the "so what" question/statement?

It didn't seem to matter how I sliced and diced the numbers on my scratchpad spreadsheet – everything had a variance. However, there was one very consistent occurrence: there was always a measurable gap between Gross Potential Rent and Stated Lease Rent. Always. And the number was sometimes double digit. Second, Collections were always lower (in aggregate) as the lease term diminished. Well, that's logical, but why such large variances?

The short answer is that it requires constant attention to retain asking rents in alignment with Gross Potential Rent. It's no different for retaining a quality record of collections (have a professional policy, implement and follow said policy). Renewals, same- install a system for gaining renewals far ahead of lease end dates, engage with professionalism and occasional incentives. These operational imperatives will have a dramatic impact on outcomes, namely, rental income.

This story is overtly simplistic considering the quality of property management software available in the marketplace. More and more even small property owners can access this software to run their assets. So where does RRT come in? RRT is not a replacement for a quality property management software program, professional property management or intelligent due diligence systems. It is a shortcut. A quick assessment of fact that brings disparities between the selected variables to light immediately. That is a powerful tool for owners, managers and buyers.

The answer was right in front of me all the time. Creating a simple mathematical formula allowed for repetition- with speed- in identifying where to start, about where to focus management attention to improve results.

Part 3
Rent Roll Triangle: The Nuts and Bolts

Collecting Baseline Data

Analysis of a rent roll requires having a basket of information that is property specific and collectable. Rent roll analysis begins with simple yet powerful outputs that conveys relative financial strength, or quality of income, derived from rental property. Rent Roll analysis with RRT pinpoints areas of financial weakness at the operational level. Knowing the strength of income and areas of weakness allows the operator (or owner, or investor) to pinpoint where to focus attention thereby correcting weaknesses sooner. These corrections should in turn increase the quality of the income stream.

Baseline data is information gathered by your team to provide a comparison of facts received from ownership or management.

Baseline data is fact–based information used in the creation of the rent roll. Baseline data is everything collected to insert into the rent roll with the objective of validating rental income. Baseline data includes property and financial information provided from sources other than the seller or seller's representative. Baseline data includes the following information:

- Income (per in-place leases)
- Vacancy (as a validator of GPR for the subject asset)
- Address
- Built Square Feet

Income is rental income as derived exclusively from rental payments from the lease file review. In constructing the rent roll for use with RRT, exclude ancillary income sources: <u>look at just rents</u>. As rents represent most income from rental property, this is where to focus your attention on the income side.

Vacancy. For baseline data purposes, what is vacancy as a percentage of occupied space and in-place leases? This is the "check point" in the review of occupancy. In your purse review stand with the weeds and focus on gross rentable space comparing this to total space leased. The drill down to undeniable facts with the lease file review or lease abstract.

Addresses are important and this is the time to check (and double check) that the legal address as described by the seller and sellers' representatives matches the on-site address. Fraud can be found everywhere sale of rental property this no exception. As I've said in other parts of the book the money invested it Is likely your own. That said it's not always someone else's responsibility to check the smallest of facts: such as what address are we buying and does it match municipal records.

Built Square Feet is the total number of square feet under roof. As a reasonable starting point, allow the rent roll to calculate rent per square foot from "built square feet". As necessary, the numbers can break the space down to rentable, common areas, administrative and storage space, etc.

Rent roll analysis is time-consuming. Breaking down the work into sections, beginning with the collection of baseline data, makes the work that much easier and efficient. Having total built square feet provides a number to determine the square footage that is revenue-producing as a percentage of total square feet.

Building Blocks of RRT (The Triangle)

There are four components to creating and completing RRT analysis; gross potential rents, stated rental revenue per in–place leases, actual collections and lease term. One variable, gross potential rents, is obtained from the market data where the property competes. The other three variables are specific to the asset. The triangle represents the three property specific variables.

- Stated Lease Rent (SLR – stated rents per in–force leases)
- Collected Rent (CR – actual collections)
- Lease Term (LT – percent of lease term fulfilled)

These variables in the RRT calculation are the "keys to the kingdom" in terms of determining quality and strength of income for a rental property. When performing acquisitions due diligence, collecting data points at the beginning of the property review process and running the RRT equation provides an immediate "cut point" to consider: a real number to influence your decision about whether to devote any additional resources (real dollars in terms of time, energy and staff) in pursuit of an asset. If the review is for an owned asset the same baseline data is in use to score the asset. The same is true for comparative properties.

To restate: although there are four variables the triangle includes the three variables that are property specific. Gross Potential Rent is a market–wide measure.

Gross Potential Rents (GPR)

Gross Potential Rents (GPR) is the number that reflects the production of maximum rent daily. GPR is a present-day representation of current market rents. Regardless of in–place rents, GPR should be regularly updated to reflect current, real time, rental income potential. Consider that every vacant property has as a price target representing maximum market rent that can be obtained in a reasonable period. That highest price point can be adjusted daily. Like the price of a stock, if there are no buyers the price can adjust downward and if there are more buyers than sellers the price can adjust upward as demand increases. It is not a static number. GPR adjusts to market conditions.

Think of GPR in terms of a vending machine that dispenses cold drinks at an outside venue. As the temperature rises the price rises and as the temperature drops the price drops. The reverse would be true for a vending machine that dispenses hot drinks; as temperatures drop the price of their product increases. The elasticity of price changes with the changing market environment. This same economic paradigm plays out every day with rental asking prices.

Stated Lease Rent (SLR)

With rental property, most tenants are paying in advance for services received over the next 30 days. Rent is due on the first of the month, to pay for the next 30 days of occupancy. For purposes of rent roll analysis, you want to know how much is due, per the written contractual leases in–force, and how much was paid and when. Simple, right? It is a time value of money equation, just crunched into thirty day increments.

Does the rental income as presented by the seller represent the same rental income as reflected in a review of in–place leases? Most revenue from rental property is derived from rents, of course. The number that has the most meaning is contractual rental income. Another important number is the year-over-year percent change in rental income.

Collected Rents (CR)

The number that matters most when determining current rental income is comparing the rental amount as represented by in–place leases against actual collections. The sustainability and success of a rental property is based on collections. Strong collections come from good screening and the implementation of a sound collections policy. Collections represent the culmination of everything provided to a tenant for the right to receive funds for services rendered. Consistently low collections spell disaster. The fastest way to fail is to have a lax collection policy.

Collected Rents represent money received, as a percentage of rent due, obtained from contractual rents.

29

A collections report conveys actual collections for a given period, usually a single month. Without collecting rents services provided fall to ash as only a portion of collections is profit. Usually, collected revenue is paid out to vendors and service providers with profit reflected after all payments (including mortgage debt) "and" impounds and reserves are fully funded.

A high level of collections translates to a high-quality income stream. This is an over–simplification. It is true that a high level of "consistent collections" can infer a quality income stream. Yet even if this is the case, maintaining this level of quality requires lease documentation to validate "going forward" expectations. This is so very important because things change. Competition, market dynamics, local and national economic occurrences can create change in operational dynamics.

Collection expectations are that Stated Lease Rent (from in–place leases) and Collected Rent (actual collections) will be the same number. In the real world, these two seldom meet. There is invariably a disparity caused by a present-day event; from late payers to those that decide to pay two months in advance to people that skip out altogether. There are changes to the billed amount (rental increases) with tenants forgetting to include this in their current payment.

Lease Term (LT)

A lease is a term rental agreement. One of the many moving parts of rental property is multiple leases. Every lease has a start date and an end date; an inception and an expiration. The sole source of information for the remaining lease term is the lease itself and any in–force addendums that may extend the lease beyond its original lease term.

Lease Term: the interval between the time a lease goes into effect and its expiration.

What is the average length of in–place leases…in months? Is it 8 months or 18 months? What percentage of lease rents (per the in–places leases) is collected? Attesting to the validity of a lease requires knowing:

- The amount of rent contractually due

- The contract term (lease term and extensions)

- Payment history (collections)

This is the starting point for performing a lease abstract. By providing a competitive rental product you can anticipate a certain level of occupancy (not 100% at-all-times, of course). In residential rental property, the short duration of leases allows people to commit for a single year, making the commitment palatable.

Rental property with the least turnover, meaning a property experiencing high lease renewals (or retention) will experience less turnover costs.

The importance of lease renewals cannot be overstated. There is a direct correlation between the number of tenants that remain in place for an extended period and the profitability of the rental property.

Removing Physical "Occupancy"

Let me take a moment to answer the question about why physical occupancy is excluded from the RRT equation. How can a mathematical formula about rental income provide valid outputs without accounting for physical occupancy? The answer is that physical occupancy is accounted for when comparing Gross Potential Rents (GPR) to collections. When there are large percentage differentials between these variables you can assume that physical occupancy is a factor, certainly.

The second reason for excluding physical occupancy is because there are too many definitions: there is the abject physical occupancy, economic occupancy and financial occupancy (based on varying definitions of revenue). My underlying reason for excluding these varying definitions is because they already receive an overt amount of attention.

Including physical occupancy in the RRT calculation, I believe, provides this one variable too much weight thus effectively negating the interplay between the equation and its selected variables. In other words; occupancy is too easy. By leaving occupancy out of the equation, I am asking you to delve deeper into the elasticity of the numbers provided by the interplay of the selected variables; Gross Potential Rent, Stated Lease Rent, Collections and Lease Term.

Part 4

Rent Roll Triangle: Theory & Math

Rent Roll Triangle – Theory

The Theory

Some will ask why "the math" is at the tail end of this book rather than right up front. The reasoning is because I want you to first consider applications of the equation rather than getting lost in the equation. Granted, the order may seem a little backwards considering this book is all about "the numbers." In this case, practicality dictates that you consider the math and theory behind the calculations after an in-depth discussion of the power of the equation outputs. A more blatant reason is that any math seems to make many a person skip or just read around equations of any sort.

An upfront word about basic math rules; remember to perform multiplication or division before addition or subtraction. Work from inside brackets first, then parentheses, then do the remaining math following the basic math rules just described. I will elaborate on these rules below as they apply to the Rent Roll Triangle.

Rent Roll Triangle (RRT %) is a calculation. Analogous to the term "Iron Triangle" that is used by political scientists to describe the strong ties between Congress, Bureaucracy, and Interest Groups in the United States in matters of public policy. The RRT (%) emphasizes the strong ties between, and powers of, Stated Lease Rents, Collected Rents (collections), and the term of in-place Leases in predicting the strength of future income.

Here's how RRT (%) is calculated:

RRT (%) = ((SLR / GPR)(CR/SLR)((LT/12])/12)) X 100)

> Where "X" = multiplication and "/" = division
>
>> SLR = Stated Lease Rents
>>
>> GPR = gross potential rents (total dollars per annum)
>>
>> CR = collected rents (collections, total dollars per annum)
>>
>> LT = Lease Term (months of lease)

And, where mathematical operations inside parentheses are completed first; first regular parentheses, then bold parentheses, then outside operations

Here is an explanation:

First, RRT (%) is calculated using three factors that are not only interlocking but also can each independently affect the rent roll. For example, lease terms (LT) not only influence the RRT (%) directly, they also influence both collected rents (CR) and Stated Lease Rents (SLR). As an obvious example, a lease term (LT) of 10 months would reduce collected rents (CR) over the more ideal term of 12 months. We show these relationships in Figure 1, and express them mathematically in the un-derived form of the equation shown above.

Note that the resulting RRT (%) is expressed as a percentage. Here, I believe it would probably be best to review both the basic math involving calculation of percentages and review some of the related statistics that both allow and limit interpretation of percentages.

The Math

Although you would not know it from looking at them, percentages are a special form of fractions. Fortunately for us, we will only have to deal with simple or common mathematical fractions, not complex ones (such as ones that contain negative numbers, or irrational numbers such as square root of 2, or pi), in order to explain the uses and limitations of percentages such as the RRT (%). Common mathematical fractions are made up of two integers, one up top of a line, and another one underneath. The one up top is called the numerator, the one underneath the denominator. The denominator cannot be zero. For fractions like RRT (%), the line represents a mathematical operation, division.

Common fractions may have different uses. With one use, the integer in the denominator tells us how many parts make a whole or a unit, and the integer up top tells us how many parts are actually in that particular fraction. For example, "1/2", read "1 over 2", or "1 per 2", or "1 of 2", or "1 divided by 2", is a fraction. "One" is the numerator, "2" the denominator. From the denominator, we know that two parts would make up the whole, or the unit. From the numerator, we know that only one of the parts is present in that fraction.

A specific example might be a cinnamon bun that you cut into two equal slices. You give one slice to your significant other and keep the other one for yourself. Expressed as a common fraction, "1/2", the numerator would represent the slice you kept (or, the one you gave your significant other), and the denominator the number of slices needed to make a whole bun. And, in this example, we know from the numerator that you (or your significant other) have only one of the two parts needed to make a whole bun.

Another use of fractions, important for our understanding of RRT(%), is to express equivalence. Here, the integer in the denominator does not necessarily tell us how many parts it takes to make a whole, and the numerator does not necessarily tell us how many parts we have.

Suppose your two kids came into the kitchen just as you were slicing the cinnamon bun. After a brief discussion, you think it prudent to cut the bun into four rather than two equal slices. Two, one each for you and your significant other, and two, one each, for the kids. You can also represent the consequence of the appearance of the kids as a fraction. Now, the denominator would be four because it would take four slices to make the cinnamon bun whole again. And, the numerator would be two if it represented the number of slices among you and your significant other, or the number of slices among the kids.

The fraction would therefore be "2/4". But, notice that you could also divide the top and the bottom of the fraction by 2 (because dividing, or multiplying the top and bottom of a fraction by the same number, in this case 2/2, is the same as dividing, or multiplying, by one), resulting in the fraction "1/2". This fraction is said to be equivalent to the fraction "2/4" (as would be "3/6" or "5/10", or "500,000/1,000,000). In fact, "1/2" is also known as the "reduced" form of "2/4" (or, of the other examples shown in parenthesis). "1/2" is the fraction equivalent of "2/4", but the former fraction does not tell us the cinnamon bun is in four rather than two slices, and that the kids took off with two of them, leaving you and your significant other each with only "1/4" of the bun. In this case, we have clear theoretical mathematical equivalence, but an equally clear undesirable practical outcome (should have bought two buns). Think about how this practical outcome might apply in an unwary application of RRT (%) explained a bit further below).

As a slightly different view of the equivalence of common fractions, 1 bad apple of 2 total apples can be represented as the ratio "1/2", but so can 2 bad apples of 4 total apples, or 250 bad apples of 500 total apples. This is because both "2/4", or 250/500" can be mathematically simplified, or "reduced" to "1/2" and are therefore equivalent fractions. The former example can be reduced by dividing both numerator and denominator by 2, the latter by dividing both by 250.

In each case, one can say that there is one bad apple for every two total apples in the bags or in the cart. This is one of the great properties of fractions. They allow comparison of things that may seem, in fact may be, quite different. Whether it is 4 bad apples in a bag of 8, or 6 eggs broken in a carton of 12 or multiple 6 month leases in a year, the ratios can all be reduced to the same mathematical fraction of "1/2"!

Because fractions are often unitless (that is, cinnamon bun slices in the numerator is divided by, or "cancels out", cinnamon bun slices in the denominator, as do the apples or eggs, so the fraction itself is unitless), equivalence is an important concept to keep in mind when comparing RRT (%)s among different assets. For example, the RRT (%) may be identical, but if one asset has a GPR of $5 million per annum, and another only $50,000 per annum, the practical dollar impacts of the RRT (%) for one might be two orders of magnitude (that is, one hundred times) greater than the other!!

But, you argue, enough about fractions without some further clarification. Are percentages even fractions??? Percentages don't have denominators, as any common fraction should. Where is the denominator in 50%, or 75%, or 93%? And I agree. Percentages don't look at all like common fractions. But then, neither do decimal fractions such as 0.5 or scientific notation such 5.0 X 10-1. And, yet, each of these is also a fraction. And, in each case, the denominator is implicitly understood without being written.

In the case of decimal fractions, the denominator is understood to be an integer power of ten. For 0.5, for example, the numerator is 5 and the denominator is assumed to be 10, because there is one digit to the right of the decimal point. If the decimal fraction were written instead as 0.50, the numerator would be 50 and the denominator would be assumed as 100, because there are two digits to the right of the decimal point. Five divided by 10, or 50 divided by 100, gives the fraction 0.5. In the case of 5.0 X 10-1, the 10-1 represents a denominator of 10 because the minus one means the ten goes in denominator, again giving a fraction of 5/10, or 0.5.

Percentages represent a third type of fraction where the denominator is implied rather than written. Percentages are only slightly more complex than the other examples. And, you can blame it all on the Romans! The Romans were among the first to find that they could simplify many practical calculations by using "100" as a common denominator (hence Latin per centum, meaning "per hundred").

Roman businessmen found it useful to express some things as fractions, particularly those based on 100 as the denominator. Thus, taxes levied in Roman times might be 1 coin per 100 coins earned, or 1 sheep per 100 sheep sold. Meaning if you had 500 coins, you owed 5 coins in taxes, or, if you 600 sheep, you owed 6 of them in taxes. Just like the Romans, when we say "percent" we mean per 100. Said slightly different, we mean we are expressing our results as a fraction in which the bottom term is always 100. Thus, 1% percent means 1 per 100, 25% means 25 per 100, and 80% means 80 per 100.

As already suggested, understanding that percentages are in fact fractions is important both for their calculation and interpretation, including the RRT (%). As an illustrative example, suppose a basket has both bad and good apples in it. Suppose the basket contains exactly 100 apples. Twenty-three are bad, and seventy-seven are good. What percentage are bad? You might intuitively say that 23% are bad, and that would be correct. But how did your intuitive brain arrive at the correct percentage? Without much (maybe no) conscious effort, your brain probably did something akin to the following math,

23 bad apples / 100 total (good and bad) apples X 100% = 0.23 X 100% = 23% bad apples

Good intuitive math!!! Now, suppose the basket has only 79 apples, but 18 of these are bad. What percentage are bad? Here, unless you are a mathematical wizard, your intuitive brain will probably punt. Smart brain!! But you are in luck, because the basic equation that we used above will still work (with the help of a calculator), as below:

Eighteen bad apples/79 total apples X 100% = 0.2278 X 100% = 22.78% or about 23% bad apples.

Note several points here. One is that we round off the percentage, in this case to the nearest whole apple. But, also note that 23 bad apples in a basket containing 100 total apples is the same percentage (23%) as 18 bad apples in a basket containing only 79 total apples (also 23%). Equivalence again. That is because percentages are a form of fractions, and equivalence, as described above, is a key to understanding percentages.

Say, for example, 23% of the apples in a basket are bad. We don't necessarily know whether the basket has a total of 79, 100, or 6,000 (assume it's a big basket) apples. In equivalence talk, it simply means that 23 out of every 100 apples are bad in the basket. Or, suppose your calculation of Rent Roll Triangle (%) for an asset come out to 58%. In this case, only 58 of every 100 potential dollars is being realized, whether the asset has a total annual income of $500,000 or $25,000,000!

Now, let's revisit the basic math we just used above to calculate percentages. If you know the fraction, say its 23/100 apples are bad as in the example above, the calculation is

23 bad apples/100 total apples X 100%, or, 23%

Again, 23% simply means 23 per 100. And in this example, note that apples are the item being counted in both the numerator and the denominator. Mathematically, apples in the numerator "cancel out" the apples in the denominator. The consequence is a unitless percentage. One doesn't need a specific unit to calculate a percentage, only a fraction.

To calculate the percentage of a unit less fraction then, just take the fraction and multiply it by 100%. For example, if the fraction is 0.5, or 1/2, the percent is:

0.5 X 100 or 50% or

½ X100 or 50%

Even if the fraction is not based on one hundred, suppose the fraction is 18/83, the ratio is still multiplied by 100% to get the percentage, as below:

18/83X100 %= 21.7%

Except for a few important side notes, that hopefully should be about all you need to review about the basic calculation of a percentage for this book. One such side note: for some RRT (%) uses, it might also be helpful to know that if you know a percentage, you can calculate the related fraction. But this should be intuitively obvious, and will always result in a fraction based on one hundred as the denominator, or an equivalent. Suppose, for example, your RRT (%) calculated at 88%. From a fractional perspective, this would mean you were realizing essentially 88 dollars for every 100 potential dollars, or a fraction of 0.88. An equivalent fraction would be 44/50 (divide the numerator and the assumed denominator of 100 each by 2) or 22/25 (divide the numerator and the assumed denominator of 100 each by 4).

The reduced or equivalent fractions themselves may come in handy in your use of RRT (%) by simplifying some calculations.

Another side note: in calculating a percentage, the numerator and denominator should be the same basic item, e.g. apples or oranges, counted in the same type of units. For RRT (%), this will almost always be money, but it would be important to make sure the unit of currency in the numerator and denominator is the same. The same holds true for a basic calculation of a fraction; know that both the numerator and denominator are expressed as percentages. For example, 30% as a percentage is equivalent to 30%/100% = 0.3, but not equivalent to 30%/100 (which would be 0.003, if you calculate it).

Having reviewed the basic math to calculate a single percentage, hopefully this refresher has allowed you to consider some fundamental thoughts on how these percentages can affect change as interpreted in the world of RRT (%). Hold those thoughts for a bit later, when we look at percentages considering some basic statistics.

Right now, we have one more step in basic math of percentages that needs attention. We now know how to calculate a percentage from a single fraction, and how to make such a fraction from basic data. But, the RRT (%) is not calculated from a single percentage, it is calculated from a whole string of percentages. So, how do we accomplish that computation mathematically, and what practical information can the math behind the computation tell us about the nature of RRT (%)?

Groups of fractions, and therefore percentages, can be subjected to all basic mathematical operations including addition, subtraction, multiplication, and division. Fortunately for us, the only operation used on the three fractional factors used in computing the RRT (%) is multiplication (not counting division within the fractional factors themselves, because we have already covered that!).

To gain some insight on how to multiply fractions, and what the multiplication of fractions means, let us look at a simple case. We will start by multiplying two fractions, as exemplified below:

(1/2) X (1/3) equals ??

The math is simple: multiply the numerators together, and multiply the denominators together, as below:

(1/2) X (1/3) = (1 X1) / (2 X 3) = (1/6)

Here, using a practical example, is an interpretation of what the math might mean practically. Suppose you have just picked eighteen apples from the single tree in your back yard. Your thinking apple pie, and plan to suggest this with your significant other as soon as he or she gets home. However, you see your neighbor lady on the way back, know she loves apples and has no tree, so you give her half of them before you even make it to your back door. Now you have 9 (or 1/2). Surprise! Your daughter is waiting inside the house, visiting from the other side of town. She loves your homegrown apples, and is pleased to accept most of the remaining ones for her family. She takes two-thirds, leaving you one third of the remaining 9, or three. Let us look mathematically at what just happened:

(18 apples) X ((1/2) X (1/3)) = (18 apples) X ((1 X1) / (2 X 3)) = (18 apples) X (1/6) = 18 apples / 6 = 3 apples. Yup, time to check the tree again, or give up the pie.

From the perspective of rental income, here is how an analogous calculation might work. Suppose you are looking at a property that has a documented Gross Potential Rent of $100,000, but is only realizing half (1/2) in Stated Lease Rents, and has a Lease Term of about four months (1/3). Do the math:

($100,000 per annum) X ((1/2) X (1/3)) = ($100,000 per annum) X ((1 X1) / (2 X 3)) = ($100,000 per annum) X (1/6) = $100,000 per annum / 6 = $16,666 per annum.

Note that we portray in this example the mathematical operations a little differently than we present them in the formula for RRT (%), and note also that we neglected any information you might have gotten about actual Collected Rents. Nonetheless, we came up with a meaningful computation that might help provide an objective basis for deciding the real income potential of this proposed asset. Perhaps, based on what other information you have gathered on how the asset is advertising and managed, you are looking at a rough, uncut diamond. Or, maybe you would be better off buying more apple trees!!

Note, as stated above, that we ignored information you may have had on Collected Rents in the preceding example. We did that because we had not explicitly looked at how to do the mathematical computation for a fraction involving three rather than two factors. Let us now look at such a computation.

This time you go out to your tree, and pick all remaining ripe apples, a total of 48. Knowing you only need at least six apples for a pie, and having already negotiated the baking to be done by your significant other (you grew the apples), you figure the pie is already in the bag! But, on the way back, you see the lady next door, who is delighted that you have apples, and again takes her half (1/2), leaving you with 24 apples. And, guess who is waiting inside the house? Your daughter from the other side of town, of course. She leaves you with one-third again, this time eight apples. Still enough for the pie. Unfortunately, when your significant other begins to prepare apples for the pie, he or she notes three quarters of the apples (3/4) are severely infested with apple "bugs", and unusable. That leaves you one fourth (1/4, two.

Here is the math:

(48 apples) X ((1/2) X (1/3) X (1/4)) = (48 apples) X ((1 X1 X 1) / (2 X 3 X 4)) = (48 apples) X (1/) = 48 apples / 24 = 2 apples. Maybe you could settle for some apple dumplings??

Now, let's go back to RRT (%). Suppose, as before, you are looking at a property that has a documented Gross Potential Rent of $100,000, but is only realizing half (1/2) in Stated Lease Rents, and has a Lease Term of about four months (1/3). But, this time you also know the fraction of collect rents, which is one fourth (1/4). Now do the math:

($100,000 per annum) X ((1/2) X (1/3) X (1/4)) = ($100,000 per annum) X ((1 X1 X 1) / (2 X 3 X 4)) = ($100,000 per annum) X (1/24) = $100,000 per annum / 24 = $4,166 per annum. Nonetheless, the example illustrates how the math is done with fractions, and points to the interrelatedness of factors tied mathematically by multiplication.

Now, back to the Rent Roll Triangle (%) as presented at the beginning of this theoretical discussion, and as used in the text and examples throughout the rest of the book. The formula is presented again below:

RRT (%) = ((SLR / GPR)(CR/SLR)((LT/12])/12)) X 100)

> Where "X" = multiplication and "/" = division
>
> > SLR= Stated Lease Rents
> >
> > GPR = gross potential rents (total dollars per annum)
> >
> > CR = collected rents (collections, total dollars per annum)
> >
> > LT = Lease Term (months of lease: not to exceed 12 months)

Note that the formula is presented in a form assuming SLR, GPR, and CR are each presented in estimated or actual dollars, and that LT is presented in months. With this form, dollars "cancel out" for the first two factors, and the third factor, LT, assumes an ideal of 12 (in months).

A lease term of more than 12 months is taken as 12 for purposes of RRT. If the lease is a multi-year lease un-fulfilled, then divide the lease fulfilled by the term of the in-place lease to obtain a percent for LT.

I will illustrate using Scenario #1 from my book "How to Read a Rent Roll" (p. 138), as follows.

Consider a 300-unit multifamily apartment unit where stated lease rents (SLR) are at 90% of GPR with average rents of $900 per unit per month. The objective is to reach and maintain market rents. Remember that GPR is always a moving target as a gauge of market rents in real time moving rental increases and setting prices on available units higher or lower as the marketplace changes.

> Gross Potential Rent: GPR = $3,300,000
>
> Stated Lease Rents: SLR = $3,000,000
>
> Collected Rents: CR = $2,950,000
>
> Lease Term: LT = 12 months'

RRT (%) = ((SLR / GPR)(CR/SLR)((LT/12])/12)) X 100)

Or

RRT(%) = (($3,000,000/$3,300,000)($2,950,000/$3,000,000)((12 - [12-12])/12) X100)

= 89.39 %

Or

RRT(%) = A. ($3,000,000 / $3,300,000) = 0.90909 etc

B. ($2,950,000 / $3,000,000) = 0.98333 etc

C. ((12 - [12- 12])/12) = 1.00

= A X B X C X 100

= 0.90909 X 0.98333 X 1.00 X 100

= 89.39 %

Note several points important for getting the correct result. Each of the three factors is first converted to a fraction; the fractions are then multiplied following rules described above for computation of three fractions using multiplication; and, the consequent fraction is then multiplied by 100 to convert the fraction to percentage (per one hundred).

The second computation shows this in a slightly simplified way by labeling the factors A, B, and C. The steps are essentially the same, however, and you can see that the results of the computations are also the same.

One final point regarding the nature of percentages. Percentages are a form of data that statisticians sometimes refer to as "normalized." "Normalized" means that the data from different scales allows their comparison on a single scale. A familiar example of normalization is a student grade point average, often given on a scale from 0 to 4. Here, a school will take grades from different teachers who range broadly in how they give grades, put the grades all on the same scale, and calculate a summary grade that is assigned to the student, say 3.4 GPA for a semester, year, or total time and classes at the school.

The summary GPA is used by other schools, e. g., a university to compare likelihood of success of students who are coming from different high schools in different parts of the country and, indeed, the world. While the university would be quick to point out that they understand the high schools vary widely in how the GPAs are assigned, it at least gives an indication of how well one student may perform in the classroom as opposed to another.

The following comments are mainly for the statistically sophisticated reader. First, I remind you that two or more percentages, including RRT (%) can be compared (statistically) to determine if they are significantly different. Such information might be helpful when an investor is trying to decide which of two or more properties might be the better or best asset to acquire.

Statistical tests used include common ones such as t-tests, Chi square, or ANOVA (analysis of variance, a statistical method in which the variation in a set of observations is divided into distinct components). With these tests, you can look at the variability around the percentages, then assess whether the differences are significant within that level of variability.

Nonparametric tests (tests that do not assume the data fall within a normal or Bell shaped distribution) are often preferred over parametric tests (tests that assume the data do fall within a normal, or Bell shaped, distribution) because percentages can better meet the assumptions of nonparametric tests. For example, parametric tests assume a normal distribution and that data can roam freely between negative infinity and positive infinity. That is, values for data are unconstrained in either direction.

Percentages do not fit that assumption because they are constrained, in that they can only range between 0% and 100%. The problem is particularly acute for values close to zero or one hundred. To fix this problem, percentages are sometimes transformed into their arc sine, or logarithmic equivalents, and statistical tests performed and interpreted on the transformed data, rather than on the raw percentages.

And so, it is with the RRT (%) and rental property. RRT (%) is not an absolute value. The RRT (%) of an asset will always fall somewhere between 0% and 100%, even though GPRs may range over several orders of magnitude- say from $500 million for one potential asset- to a GPR of only $3 million for another. RRT (%) may see them both as equivalent, say 78%.

The advantage of such normalization is that it allows comparison of rent potential between real property assets that have widely disparate values. A disadvantage is that the user needs to keep in mind that 78% of $50 million is a much different amount of money than 78% of $3 million. And, while the basis for assignment of an RRT (%) may differ widely between individual properties for many reasons, the RRT (%) does provide an indication of how well one property might perform as opposed to another. It is up to the savvy investor to understand the differences.

Base Case

The following are real world scenarios in a case study format with narratives providing a diverse representation in RRT output numbers and some potential remedies to improve RRT score. The base case represents perfected revenue generation. The case studies represent varied scores using the base case calculation and applying it to different rental property scenarios.

Case studies following the base case represent "real world" scenarios with case background, a premise for the case, an RRT output number, solutions and recommendations. Solutions and recommendations are not comprehensive. They represent an initial assessment for contemplation during further study towards implementation of an action plan to improve rental income represented in the case.

The base case presumes 100% attainment for each revenue category where:

- The property is attaining 100% of GPR
- The property is collecting 100% of stated lease rents
- That collections equal 100% of stated lease rents
- That each in–place lease reaches full maturity of 12–months.

The following is the "base case" of the RRT calculation, whereas the rental property in question is operating at full potential. Please remember to always perform multiplication or division before addition or subtraction.

Gross Potential Rent: GPR = $100,000

Stated Lease Rents: SLR = $100,000 (SLR is multiplied by percent occupancy)

Collected Rents: CR = $100,000 (CR is SLR multiplied by percent collected)

Lease Term: LT = 12

RRT (%) = (SLR ÷ GPR x 100)(CR ÷ SLR x 100)
(1 − [12 − LT] ÷ 12) x 100)

= (SLR ÷ GPR)(CR ÷ SLR)(1 − [12–LT] ÷ 12 x 100)

Or

RRT (%) = (100,000 ÷ 100,000 x 100)(100,000 ÷ 100,000 x 100)
(1 − [12 − 12] ÷ 12 x 100)

= (100,000 ÷ 100,000)(100,000 ÷ 100,000)(1 − [12–12] ÷ 100)

= (100%)(100%)(100%)

= 100.00%

RRT (%) = A. (SLR ÷ GPR x 100) = 100%

B. (CR ÷ SLR x 100) = 100%

C. (1 − [12 − LT] ÷ 12) x 100) = 100%

=(100%)(100%)(100%)

=100.00%

Although redundant, please remember to perform multiplication or division before addition or subtraction.

A score of 100% does not negate the potential to grow revenue or divulge the asset is at peak: it does denote that the asset is at peak in the manner it is presently being operated. Here is an example.

A small strip center in an up-and-coming part of town has a bail bond, tax preparer and nail salon as tenants. The owners assess recent changes in demographics and conclude a different tenant mix is imperative. They bring in a cell phone service provider, a specialty pizza store and wine shop. As the three in-coming tenants all have higher margins than the out-going tenants the lease rates will likely be higher. It's all about what the demographics will support: changes in demographics bring changes in potential lease rates.

Part 5
Rent Roll Triangle Case Studies

Four variables make up the data sets used in RRT; the three property specific corners making up the triangle plus the market data from Gross Potential Rent. Here is an abridged definition of each variable in the equation.

Gross Potential Rent (GPR). GPR represents a perfect world whereas every rentable square foot is 100% occupied all the time with never a single day of vacancy for any reason. GPR also presumes 100% collections for the entire year.

Stated Lease Rent is the lessee's representation of rental income derived from an income–producing real estate asset. This is validated by a review of individual lease files to correlate documentation with outcomes presented in the rent roll

Collected Rent refers to the funds received for rents due; funds received, obtained and banked on behalf of the property. Collected rent is money received, as a percentage of rent due, from contractual rental income for contractual rents.

Lease Term is the interval between the time a lease is in affect and its expiration date. Identifying the average length of tenancy is a significant determinant of tenant stability.

The following case studies are presented to wrap some realism around the theory. Each is a synopsis rather than a soup to nuts solution for the asset described. RRT is inherently about rental revenue. RRT excludes factors related to the age of a property, its condition or location.

RRT is a starting point to identify further actions necessary to remedy gaps in revenue between GPR, SLR and CR. RRT does not consider physical property attributes, age, deferred maintenance, traffic counts or new competition entering the marketplace. While these are of consideration by the serious investor, the calculation is void of any representation about such. At the same time, a lower score versus a higher score will invariably tie back into the condition of the asset, its market and how it competes with competitive assets.

Many assets will be shooting towards attaining a higher RRT score from a current operational stanza that will benefit from professional property management and implementing actions that drive revenue. For assets with scores nearing 100% the RRT representation is that the asset is near maximum revenue potential <u>as the asset is presently operated.</u> Changes to operational strategy, which in turn changes GPR, requires a new RRT calculation taking into consideration the new operational persona.

The Case study format provides a forum for reviewing various types of rental property real estate to see how they interact with the formula. Every investor has a different set of eyes. Depending on how you intend to use RRT, consider each case from the perspective of: a potential acquisition candidate, an owned asset, for reviewing comparable assets or as an asset manager or property manager.

Case studies can be rather boring. Static. Good only for reading before you go to sleep. Let me know if you change that idea. Presume that every dollar in every deal within these case studies belongs to you. Read them with that in mind and they will present themselves in a whole new light. Everyone knows there is such a thing is dumb money and everyone presumes those dollars belong to someone else. As you're aware, the only thing more difficult than making money it's keep. Think of these case studies, in the RRT formula, as one more layer of protection for your dollars invested into real estate equity.

Set your "vision" in your mind and review the case from that perch. Are you a buyer? Bring a buyer's view to the case studies. After this "vision" move over to using RRT for comparable assets- applying the same technique to the subject asset (the asset under consideration) and competitive properties. Here, "competitive" has a Y in the road: competitive assets for your investment dollars and directly competitive assets in the marketplace of the subject asset. Be sure to segregate outcomes to avoid confusion days or weeks later when the information comes back around for review by others on your team.

If using RRT from an owner or property management "vision", keep that hat on throughout your reading of the case studies. What would you do/add/ change from the case from an owner or property management perspective to improve operational outputs to increase revenue? I have provided a "first cut" solutions and recommendation response. In your case, as an owner or property manager, you know your assets; their idiosyncrasies, their warts, hairline cracks, super positives, their competitors. Use this proprietary knowledge and impute that information into your very own case study for each owned or management asset. What is the background, the premise? What are our property-specific recommendations that are actionable? Write down your solutions and recommendations.

Property Type: Office Building

Case Background Information:

The property is a three-story Suburban office building with 50,000 rentable square feet of good construction and ample parking. The façade is modern and blends well with neighboring properties. Recent improvements make the property energy efficient. The property has good street visibility, is close to restaurant's and major freeways. The area attracts a young workforce because of the synergies in nearby businesses.

Premise:

The asset has remained 80% occupied for several years. Newer product continues to enter the market obtaining rents of $18 per square foot. The subject asset has in-place leases at $14 per square foot with asking rents of $17 at renewal. The average lease term is 5-years. Rents are 98% collected. Solve for RRT.

RRT Inputs:

   Gross Rent Potential = $900,000

   Stated Lease Rents = $560,000

   Collected Rents = $548,800

   Lease Term = 5 years

Solve for RRT:

RRT(%) = A. $(560,000 \div 900,000) = .6222\%$

   B. $(548,800 \div 560,000) = .9800\%$ (CR is SLR multiplied by percent collected)

   C. $(1 - [12 - 12] \div 12) \times 100) = 100\%$

   $= (.6222\%)(.9800\%)(100\%)$

   $= .6096\%$

RRT Output: 60.96%

Simplified:

RRT (%) = ((CR / GPR)(LT/12])/12) X 100)

With the following example, this shortened form is as follows:

    Gross Potential Rent: GPR = $900000

    Collected Rents: CR = $548,000

    Lease Term: LT = 12 months'

RRT (%) = (($548,000/$900,0000)((12 - [12-12])/12) X 100)

      = .6088%

      = 60.88%

Solutions and Recommendations:

This scenario is common in commercial office. In lean times, owners and managers are willing to sacrifice price for occupancy when some income is better than no income during a race to the bottom price-point to gain a lease from paying customers. When jobs go away, as occurs in times of economic difficulties, office buildings are the first to feel the pain. As businesses shrink and reduce overhead they are also reducing head counts.

When head counts decrease, so too does the need for office space. The most common measure is total number of FTE (Full Time Employee) staff. This accounts for office space use whereas there may be the same or even more actual people on payroll, however, the total number of hours worked is less thereby reducing the amount of space required to house employees considering fewer hours worked and staggered work shifts (fitting more people into less office space).

One of the underlying assumptions is that at current rents the property is covering existing expenses and debt service. If the owner has no financial pressure to make changes, then there is a lack of urgency to make dramatic changes in pursuit of increasing current value. Let's face it- not everyone needs the money and for a select few the increase in revenue can be a headache. While most of us are not in that number, this comment intends to spur your thinking as to why some buildings languish at far less than peak capacity.

Given the long-term nature of leased office space, a building locked into long-term leases at below market rent relinquishes future upside potential until lease renewal. As represented in this transaction, the upside has arrived without the building having an opportunity to capture the rental gains occurring.

Assuming multiple tenants, a review of the lease abstracts will provide a timeline on the term of each lease. Determining some leases representing a sizeable percentage of the leased space are expiring sooner rather than later, initially, will drag down RRT even more, but that information should be built-in to a plan of action to increase rents sooner. This is a representation of how fluid commercial real estate assets are in terms of requiring forward planning to maximize performance.

Waiting out existing leases will be an expensive proposition as keeping them assures a continued significant loss-to-lease from current GPR. Unlocking value in this asset requires accelerating leases as one alternative to gaining access to a larger "foot print" of available space. While this idea may seem arbitrary, not every existing tenant is looking to remain for the entire term of his or her lease. The best way to find out is to ask. Letting an existing tenant out of their lease negates a potential buyout to remove them from their current office quarters.

Depending on what new tenants are looking for, it may make sense to re-locate an existing tenant to another space in the building (and pay for the move) to free up an entire floor for a newly acquired tenant that needs space continuity.

Property Type: 48 Units Workforce Housing

Case Background Information:

This 48-unit multifamily asset is in a working-class neighborhood where median resident income is 25% less than in the metro area. There is good public transportation and elevated incidents of crime.

Working class neighborhoods have as their mainstay "workforce housing" developments as a primary form of rental housing. These developments are substantially functional but with deferred maintenance apparent. Credit quality of residents is diminished and turnover is usually higher than for A and B class assets. Many workforce housing households fall between 60% and 120% of the median household income.

Premise:

Asking rents are 13% below market. Occupancy is 85% with 90% collections. Several units are not inhabitable. There is easy-to-spot deferred maintenance. Most residence lease month-to-month with average tenancy being 9 months. Solve for RRT.

RRT Inputs:

Gross Rent Potential = $489,600

Stated Lease Rents = $362,059

Collected Rents = $325853

Lease Term = 9 months

Solve for RRT:

RRT (%) = A. (362,859 ÷ 489,600) = .7394%

B. (318,362 ÷ 362,059) = .8999% (CR is SLR multiplied by percent collected)

C. $(1 - [12 - 9] \div 12) \times 100) = .7500\%$

= (.7394%)(.8990%)(.7500%)

= .4990%

RRT Output: 49.90%

Simplified:

RRT (%) = ((CR / GPR)(LT/12])/12) X 100)

With the following example, this shortened form is as follows:

Gross Potential Rent: GPR = $489,600

Collected Rents: CR = $325,853

Lease Term: LT = 12 months'

RRT (%) = (($325,853/$489,600)((12 - [12-9])/12) X 100)

= .4991%

= 49.91%

<u>Solutions and Recommendations:</u>

This is a typical low-end rental property scenario. The first order of business is to remedy blatant deferred maintenance with nominal cash outlay, addressing the easiest-to-correct matters first followed by getting any off-line units back on line. Start with removing non-functioning vehicles, picking up trash/glass and other debris, fixing windows, doors, changing all non-functioning exterior lighting fixtures (read- install new bulbs). Identify who is leaving trash and send written warnings are impending fees is the behavior continues. Do the same for pet owners not picking up after their pets. Install on-site property management- even if only temporarily- on different days of the week. Inforce the collection policy and implement a fair and even collections methodology property-wide (applied the same to all residents).

With smaller assets, the cost burden of having on-site management is often out of reach. There are simply no economies of scale to support full-time staff on-site. Yet, if possible, this is the best thing that could happen on a small asset, the presumption being that management is trained and accomplishes their job professionally. Bringing in sub-par on-site management will not help in turning the asset around.

More than just about anything else, residents want to know that someone cares- management, ownership, someone they can rely on to follow through in maintaining a safe and decent living space and someone willing to respond, in a timely manner, to problems and maintenance calls. Once the trash is picked up and the cars are removed the mere act of starting on exterior maintenance brings a sense of caring from residents. While visibility is important, visible improvements are noticed by all.

RRT points to the fact that as much as occupancy is important, length of tenancy is a significant factor in attaining revenue goals. The most important "change event" that can occur in this case study is addressing the credit quality of residents and moving people from month-to-month to annual leases. While this will take some time to implement this change provides a huge boost to income as the length of lease improves from 9 to 12 months.

So much of workforce housing inventory has significant deferred maintenance. This is why it is important to make sure your projected market rents are "real" for the asset in question. In this case study, market rents are presumed to be more than 25% higher than stated rents. Thus, any marketing campaign will be built around methods to attain GRP and accomplish necessary property upgrades to get there.

What is the "costs to cure" to reach Gross Potential? The only reason to shoot for Gross Potential, and spend the redevelopment dollars to get there, is because ownership and management has a high level of confidence that the Gross Potential number determined is real and not a pipe dream along with believing that property improvements and quality management can reach that target.

Part of the discussion will also include a remedy for any off-line units, those units un-rented for an extended period of time (if any). If there are non-rentable units; why are they not in-service and what is necessary (in terms of costs) to make them ready to rent? And how fast can this occur, given financial constraints?

Property Type: Residential Duplex

Case Background Information:

This duplex is in an upscale neighborhood dominated by single-family homes. The rental garners premium rents because of easy access to parks, shopping and job centers. The property has long-term residents and a good landlord relationship.

Premise:

The owners have contacted a real estate broker about selling the asset with a pre-determined price point they have long suspected was within reach. The broker informs them that while similar properties have sold in that range, the value of their asset is substantially less. The broker conveys that markets rents are substantially higher than what the owner is obtaining, but provides no guidance on how to remedy or approach presumed value.

In-place rents are $1,100 monthly for each unit with residents' average lease terming being 36 months. Similar units with upgrades are renting for $1,750 a month. Solve for RRT. The property is experiencing 100% occupancy and 100% collections.

RRT Inputs:

    Gross Rent Potential = $63,000

    Stated Lease Rents = $39,600

    Collected Rents = $39,600
                    (CR is SLR multiplied by percent collected)

    Lease Term = 36

Solve for RRT:

RRT(%) = A. $(39,600 \div 63,000) = .6285\%$

        B. $(39,600 \div 39,600) = 100.00\%$

        C. $(1 - [12 - 36] \div 12) \times 100) = 100.00\%$

      = $(.6285\%)(100\%)(100\%)$

      = $.62.85\%$

RRT Output: 62.85%

Simplified:

RRT (%) = $((CR / GPR)(LT/12])/12) \times 100)$

With the following example, this shortened form is as follows:

    Gross Potential Rent: GPR = $63,000

    Collected Rents: CR = $39,600

    Lease Term: LT = 12 months'

RRT (%) = $(($39,600/$63,000)((12 - [12-12])/12) \times 100)$

      = $.6285\%$

      = 62.85%

Solutions and Recommendations:

This is an important case study, as it reflects that we can solve for RRT with no knowledge of market value. This is important because it denotes that market rents are a driver of value. In this example, the differential between current rents and market rents is huge- $650 per month per unit. Thus, it is paramount to know market rents, as is reflected in this case study; it doesn't matter if Stated Lease Rents and Collected Rents are in perfect order IF they are a football field away from market rents. This being the case, RRT delivers an output that states there is a value creation opportunity here considering the distance between current RRT and the potential for garnering a higher output score with rents closer to GPR.

To capture market value, the owner must move lease rents towards market rents. If there is no urgency to sell, then this can be accomplished over time. With rents this far under market it makes us think there must be some cause. This is a common occurrence with smaller properties- the owners could be perfectly happy with on-time rents and hassle-free tenants. Do they need another reason to keep rents so low? Of course not, unless they wish to sell. And why is the average term of tenancy so long? Because the residents know they have a GREAT deal...so who wouldn't stay if they could?

Preparing this asset for a market sale requires ownership to maximize rents. The fastest way is to send a notice of non-renewals to all residents. The letter will inform them that they must move at the expiration of their lease. There will be no lease renewal offered. To make this occur sooner, the owner may offer them cash or credit prior to the end of the lease.

With the property vacated, the owner can perform necessary upgrades to garner market rents. This can range from simple painting and cleaning to a major property rehabilitation. It is important to keep in mind that upgrades much correlate with capturing market rate rents. Post re-hab, leasing the property at market rate should have a positive impact on value and substantially raise RRT.

Property Type: 200 Units Class B Multifamily

Case Background Information:

The asset is a quality multifamily property that has changed hands three times in the last five years. Each new owner makes improvements to the property with a focus on maximizing rents. There are 80 one-bedrooms and 120 two-bedrooms with Gross Potential Rents of $900 for one-bedrooms and $1,400 for two-bedrooms.

Premise:

Management turnover and competition for customers has made for inconsistent rents, net of concessions, inconsistent maintenance, and low renewal rates with only 50% of residents renewing at the end of their lease. This has led to high turnover expenses as compared to historic norms.

The "max rent" policies with significant concessions have resulted in rents for the same unit type ranging from $800 to $1,300. One-bedroom rents average $825 and $1,250 for two-bedrooms. Occupancy is 93%, collections are 94% with an average lease term of 11 months.

RRT Inputs:

Gross Rent Potential = $240,000

Stated Lease Rents = $200,880

Collected Rents = $188,827

(CR is SLR multiplied by percent collected)

Lease Term = 11 months

Solve for RRT:

RRT (%) = A. (200,880 ÷ 240,000 X 100) = .8370%

B. (188,827 ÷ 200,880 X 100) = .9399% (CR is SLR multiplied by percent collected)

C. (1 − [12 − 11] ÷ 12) X 100) = .9167 %

= (.8370%)(.9399%)(.9167%)

= .7212%

RRT Output: 72.12%

Simplified:

RRT (%) = ((CR / GPR)(LT/12])/12) X 100)

With the following example, this shortened form is as follows:

Gross Potential Rent: GPR = $240,000

Collected Rents: CR = $188,827

(assumes no change in collections %)

Lease Term: LT = 12 months'

RRT (%) = (($188,827/$240,000)((12 - [12-11])/12) X 100)

= .7211%

= 72.11%

Solutions and Recommendations:

Consistency in lease pricing, a sincere focus on renewals, and conveying that maintenance is part of the customer service initiative of management; these three management objectives will bring an immediate positive revenue event to this asset. One of the causes for the high turnover is resident sentiment; residents talk. Residents know that the asset is being "bought and sold" based on changes in management and the lack of operational consistency.

With management presenting a message of consistent service going forward, this single item will have a dramatic impact on the renewal rate (if only 10% - that's a 20% increase in renewals~!). Presenting a consistent product will provide comfort to current residents that change-over will be "calming down." This needs to be supported by a consistent message that residents can expect a quality customer service experience going forward.

Because turnover is so high, there is opportunity to create and implement a pricing policy for moving rents towards GPR immediately. Case background tells us there is no deferred maintenance to address—the primary matter here is delivery of quality property management services for ownership that marches occupancy and rents towards max numbers consistently and methodically versus half on/half off customer care.

Management may purposefully create some turnover as they remove slow paying residents to improve overall on-time collections. So, occupancy could see a momentary dip as management strengthens leasing standards. With these operational barriers to higher income addressed management can focus their attention on attaining higher occupancy with quality residents.

Property Type: Retail Strip Center

One significant difference between residential and commercial property is lease term. With commercial property, the lease term is usually in multi-year increments. To "solve for" lease term, you must know the normalized lease term for the property type and use that as the baseline data point. Here is an example:

This property is a retail strip center of 13,500 square feet with various storefront sizes. Each space has leases with multiple 3-year increments. Thus, the in-place lease is a 3-year lease and each lease extension (pre-negotiated at the very beginning of the initial lease term) is for an additional 3-year term.

How do we solve for RRT? In this example, you know the average lease term is three years. A review of the leases for this asset will express the average term of tenancy for the existing tenants.

- What is the average length of tenancy of in-place tenants?
- Is this average term higher or lower than the presumed 3-year term?

If in-place leases average 42-months in duration, then 42/36 equals 1.17. This means that, on average, tenants remain in place 17% longer than the normalized lease term of 3-years. However, when solving for lease term in the RRT equation, the lease term component is 1.0. With smaller properties it can be common for tenants to request a few extra months to move. Owners allow this because they sometimes require additional time to find the next tenant. It is an over-simplification to say the lease term end dates, while specific, are subject to change when the parties are agreeable.

This is just one example. Average lease terms can be in 5-year increments. Sometimes leases have one-year extensions past the initial lease term. There is much variability by property type and region.

Case Background Information:
This strip center is a newer property with 13,500 square feet of leasable space. Every lease is for five-years with each tenant paying $24 per square foot with 90% occupancy and 95% on-time collections. Three years into

68

the lease term the owner is asking management for an estimate of value. Market rents are now at $21 per square foot.

Premise:

Each tenant has a five-year extension beyond the original lease with a $2 per square foot increase.

RRT Inputs:

Gross Rent Potential = $324,000

Stated Lease Rents = $291,600

Collected Rents = $277,020

(CR is SLR multiplied by percent collected)

Lease Term = 3 years

Solve for RRT:

RRT(%) = A. $(291,600 \div 324,000 \times 100) = .9000\%$

B. $(277,020 \div 291,600 \times 100) = .95.00\%$

C. $(1 - [12 - 14] \div 12) \times 100) = 100.00\%$

$= (.9000\%)(.9500\%)(100.00\%)$

$= .8550$

RRT Output: 85.50%

Simplified:

RRT (%) = ((CR / GPR)(LT/12])/12) X 100)

With the following example, this shortened form is as follows:

Gross Potential Rent: GPR = $324,000

Collected Rents: CR = $277,020

(assumes no change in collections %)

Lease Term: LT = 12 months'

RRT (%) = (($277,20/$324,000)((12 - [12-12])/12) X 100)

$= .8550\%$

$= 85.50\%$

70

Solutions and Recommendations:

While this looks to be a stellar RRT outcome, the cause is falling market rents. Still, it puts ownership on notice that there is a changing dynamic for them to be aware of and address in their decision-making process with respect to operations and lease renewals.

This is a high-quality asset (from an income generation perspective). Recognizing that the market is softening and lease rates are decreasing, it is in the best interest of ownership to obtain commitments with current tenants at the pre-determined rates for the extension period. Ownership may offer concessions in non-cash forms to retain the contract rates.

Ownership will need to make an assessment regarding late paying tenants; is it better to retain the existing late-payers at the higher lease rate or bring in new tenants (with better credit quality) at the current, yet lower, market rate? It is easy to say go for the better credit. The reality is removing slow paying tenants in hope of replacing them with higher credit quality takes time.

What if it takes a year of zero income to re-lease at lower rates and with higher credit tenants? Did this solve anything? Long-term, yes. But the in getting there is more than most owners would be willing to stand for and most could not rationally consider a year with zero rents. That's the nature of our business sentiment with banks requiring monthly updates and investors requiring quarterly returns. Such is life in non-institutional commercial real estate.

Property Type: Land Lease

In the United States, swap meets represent another shopping choice for purchasing goods and services. People love a good bargain, and swap meets are a great place to go for a family outing of bargain hunting in search of quality goods at low prices.

One of the fundamental drivers of the price of merchandise at swap meets is low overhead. The commitment by the vendor is short term, with no utilities, insurance, or other costs associated with a fixed location. In theory, lower overhead allows for part of the savings to be passed to the consumer. A win/win.

Swap meet operators over the years have become far more sophisticated. In larger markets with thriving swap meets vendors are required to make long-term commitments and sign a lease for a specific space allocation within the swap meet. Like any other real estate, some spaces have a higher value than others, usually based on pedestrian traffic.

An extreme example is the conversion of the Orange County California fairgrounds from an atypical fairgrounds and occasional swap meet location to a full-blown, every weekend swap meet generating multiple millions of dollar-a-year in leasing fees. The result is that the land that was rented by the "facility" is now being rented by the square foot. At the end of the day, it's still a lease for a specified location for a certain amount of time.

Case Background Information:
A small city has a successful summer Farmers Market for twelve Saturdays each summer. The city allows up to 50 vendors per day- first come, first serve. The land area is 2 acres and vendors are charged a flat rate of $200 per season.

There is a small parking structure next to the Farmer's Market that is being torn down to make way for a hi-rise parking structure. The new development will take up less land and offer more parking while freeing up two additional acres of ground the city can use for the farmers' market while development opportunities are considered.

The city intends to formalize the leasing process and increase fees to cover the cost of insurance and traffic management. The intensions are to have up to 100 vendors and charge a flat rate of $500 per season paid up front, non-refundable. Initial responses from potential tenants is showing strong demand. (See discussion about lease term beyond 12 months in case study for Retail Strip Center- the same applies here also).

RRT Inputs:

Gross Rent Potential = $91,000

Stated Lease Rents = $52,500

Collected Rents = $50,000

Lease Term = 12 weeks

Solve for RRT:

RRT(%) = A. (50,000 ÷ 91,000 X 100) = .5494%

B. (52,500 ÷ 50,000 X 100) = 1.050% (CR is SLR multiplied by percent collected)

C (1 − [12 − 12] ÷ 12) X 100) = 100.00 % (in this case study only weeks is equivalent to months)

= (.5494%)(1.050%)(100%)

= .5769

RRT Output: 57.69%

Simplified:

RRT (%) = ((CR / GPR)(LT/12])/12) X 100)

With the following example, this shortened form is as follows:

Gross Potential Rent: GPR = $91,000

Collected Rents: CR = $50,000

Lease Term: LT = 12 months'

RRT (%) = (($50,000/$91,000)((12 - [12-12])/12) X 100)

= .5769%

= 57.69%

Solutions and Recommendations

This is basically a land lease for a public purpose. There is revenue generated for the owner (the city) at low lease rates for purposes of increasing public participation by vendors. Yet, there are still costs associated with delivering this service: insurance, clean up, security and traffic control.

A city website can be set up to allow vendors to "confirm" their space from week-to-week. Vendors will come to the website and "confirm" on Tuesday that they will be at the site the following Saturday. It could be that a tomato vendor, while having a 12 weeks' lease, only shows up for the last eight weeks based on product availability. Unused spaces become available on Thursday for use at a rate of $150 for a single Saturday. If 80 of 100 vendors confirm, then the city has 20 spaces available that week.

To solve for Gross Potential Rent, if all 100 spaces are sold out at the beginning of the season at $500 each, revenue generated is $50,000. However, if on average 20% of the spaces are made available each week at the single day rate- and all 20 are leased at that rate: then there is added revenue potential of $36,000 ($150 per Saturday X 20 spaces X 12 weeks).

For income projection purposes, the city would have to refer to historic records. In this case study, however, there is newly available lease space previously unavailable. And in terms of what percentage of lessors will show up every week, what vacant inventory will be for single-day usage, this is in the hands of management in terms of how to market the space and make the public aware of its availability. Single-day lease rates may change significantly (up or down) depending on identified demand.

Property Type: Light Industrial Building

Case Background Information:

Light industrial buildings are used for producing and delivering consumer goods and services. Examples are auto-repair shops, Design-build contractors, print shops and home electronics installers. Compare this to heavy industrial facilities that are used to produce goods for business such as components for automobiles, appliances manufacturing and steel mills.

For purposes of obtaining an RRT for light industrial the variable to isolate is lease term as this varies widely by region. Once the normalized lease-term for the region is determined this is baseline information for comparison to the lease terms in-place at the subject property against this baseline. For purposes of this case study we presume a normalized lease term of 5 years with market rents of $6 per square foot per year.

Premise:

This is a 10,000-square foot light industrial building occupied by three commercial tenants. The property is 100% occupied with 98% collections. Market rents are $6 per square foot. One tenant has 5,000 square feet at rental rate of $3. One tenant rents 3,000 square feet at $5 and the third rents 2,000 square feet for $7.

RRT Inputs:

   Gross Rent Potential = $60,000

   Stated Lease Rents = $44,000

   Collected Rents = $43,120

   Lease Term = 5 years

Solve for RRT:

RRT(%) = A. (44,000 ÷ 60,000 X 100) = .7333%

   B. (43,120 ÷ 44,000 X 100) = .9800%

   C. (1 – [12 – 12] ÷ 12) X 100) = 100.00 % → another five
      years matter to consider

   = (.7333%)(.9800%)(100%)

   = .7186%

RRT Output: 71.86%

Simplified:

RRT (%) = ((CR / GPR)(LT/12])/12) X 100)

With the following example, this shortened form is as follows:

   Gross Potential Rent: GPR = $60,000

   Collected Rents: CR = $43,120 (assumes no change in collections %)

   Lease Term: LT = 12 months'

RRT (%) = (($43,120/$60,000)((12 - [12-12])/12) X 100)

   = .7186%

   = 71.86%

<u>Solutions and Recommendations:</u>

Two of three tenants are paying lease rates below market. One tenant is paying above market rate for a smaller space. Unlocking both greater revenue and greater value requires a change to the leases of tenants paying less than market rates. It is common practice for negotiations about extending lease terms to occur in the last year of the existing lease.

In this case study, management may consider beginning that process sooner to learn the lessor's intentions. Perhaps the tenant was planning to stay longer until they are made aware of the new higher lease rates. Future incentives could be offered to change the lease terms now, or conversely, incentives offered to vacate sooner to make way for a higher paying customer. While that may seem to be outside of the norm, considering the differential between GPR and SLR is almost 27%, ownership has cause to consider creative methods to capture this differential. The one tenant paying only $3 on 5,000 square feet is locking up $15,000 potential in annual income, representing 25% of GPR.

Property Type: 100 Unit Student Housing Developments

Case Background Information:

Freshman Manor is a 100-unit student housing development steps from a major university campus. The development has state-of-the-art amenities and no parking. There are ten studio apartments, twenty-one-bedrooms, thirty-five two-bedroom apartments and thirty-five three bedroom apartments.

Many student housing developments rent "by the bedroom". This development has 205 bedrooms to lease when including the studios as a SRO (single-residency occupant). So, in one respect student assets are unique because of leasing individual bedrooms within a single unit, yet they are not unique because the underlying occupancy is still based on a percentage of total units (beds) available for lease. Property management, while having only 100 units is managing 205 potential leases on property to gain full occupancy.

Premise:

Leasing activity focuses on fall move-ins. Over eighty percent of all new leases begin in the fall with the other twenty percent spread out over the rest of the year.

The property remains consistently 90% occupied. There is seldom a vacancy in the studio or one-bedrooms. The two-bedrooms will have some vacancy with the bulk of the vacancy being in the three-bedrooms. Asking rents are as follows:

Studio = $1,100

One-Bed = $1,300

Two-bed = $900 per bedroom

Three-bed = $800 per bedroom

RRT Inputs:

Gross Rent Potential: $2,052,000

Studio = $132,000

One-bed = $156,000

Two-bed = $756,000

Three-bed = $1,008,000

Stated Lease Rents: $1,846,800

Collected Rents: $1,772,928

Lease Term: 12 months

Solve for RRT:

RRT(%) = A. $(1,846,800 \div 2,052,000 \times 100) = .9000\%$

B. $(1,772,928 \div 1,846,800 \times 100) = .9600\%$

C. $(1 - [12 - 12] \div 12) \times 100) = 100.00\%$

= $(.9000\%)(.9600\%)(100.00\%)$

= $.8640\%$

RRT Output: 86.40%

Simplified:

RRT (%) = ((CR / GPR)(LT/12])/12) X 100)

With the following example, this shortened form is as follows:

    Gross Potential Rent: GPR = $2,052,000

    Collected Rents: CR = $1,772,928

    Lease Term: LT = 12 months'

RRT (%) = (($1,772,928/$2,052,000)((12 - [12-12])/12) X 100)

     = .8640

RRT = 86.40%

<u>Solutions and Recommendations:</u>
In recent years, operators of student housing developments have a permanent pain-in-their-neck from having to always look over their shoulder from chronic over-supply. Concurrent with the explosion of college student debt, there is and was a similar explosion in the quantity of upscale student housing developments. Private sector student housing is also in competition with newly constructed on-campus housing. Some small colleges, for purposes on "controlling the environment" while increasing university revenue have taken to requiring students to live on campus- some for two years and some for all four years in pursuit of a college degree.

With this backdrop, as with some of the other case studies presented herein, note that this is a specialty asset class that operates within a management structure very specific to the asset class (like medical office and refrigerated storage); it isn't as easy as it looks!

Student assets will deploy lease revenue optimization (LRO) software to assist management in dynamic pricing to fill vacancies. Like vending machines changing prices based on inventory and the heat index, LRO assists student property managers in changing their price targets to take advantage of demand to maximize revenue when leasing activity is robust and capture incremental gains in occupancy during the off season.

Property Type: Marina

Case Background Information:
Marina's rent space both long-term and short-term on water. A marina's as property rental facilities is well documented. Marinas are smaller than ports and do not handle large ships or passenger ship traffic. Their bread and butter is yachts, small boats and sail boats (a yacht is known as a medium sized sailboat with built-in equipment for cruising or racing on water). Marinas can be found on ocean coast, on lakes and large rivers. Some marinas are seasonal.

Many marina's offer additional boating services beyond just docking: fuel, repairs, cleaning and restoration, moving and storage. Some offer covered docks that rent for a premium. Available leased docks at marinas include annual and seasonal leases, daily and weekly rates. Some offer free daily or over-night docking with the purchase of goods or services from the marina

Premise:
The marina has a new owner, a young couple that have decided to leave the big city and make a sleepy little cove their home. They purchased the only marina for fifty miles and intend to work hard at becoming a runaway success. The locals are skeptical. While the marina has a long history nothing much has changed. The property is in good shape and has newer equipment, but traffic is light in the off season and every slip is already occupied by locals.

The summer season is just a month away and the new owners need to lay out a game plan to generate additional revenue. They find out that it is nearly impossible to get a liquor license, however, a business can obtain a thirty-day renewable permit to sell beer and wine. And although there is no kitchen equipment, they can cook and sell prepared foods from a gas grill and refrigerated side dishes with a small conversion to the office.

There are one hundred slips. Each is rented year-round at a flat rate of $1,000 with no vacancy. The new owners decide to not renew twenty leases and have these slips available for short-term, weekend and daily rental. Revenue generation for these rentals is projected to generate

RRT Inputs:

   Gross Rent Potential = $100,000

   Stated Lease Rents = $100,000

   Collected Rents = $98,100

   Lease Term = 1 year

Solve for RRT:

RRT(%) = A. $(100,000 \div 100,000 \times 100) = 100\%$

   B. $(98,100 \div 100,000 \times 100) = .998\%$

   C. $(1 - [12 - 12] \div 12) \times 100 = 100.00\%$

   $= (100\%)(.9810\%)(100\%)$

   $= .9810\%$

RRT Output: 98.10%

<u>Solutions and Recommendations:</u>
This is an example of a property where the status quo is not only boring but negates upside potential. The new owners decide to not renew twenty leases and have these slips available for short-term, weekend and daily rental. They estimate each will rent for $2,000 for the season with some vacancy. Revenue generation for these rentals is projected to generate $38,000.

With $2,000 in equipment, some picnic tables and umbrellas they open a weekend restaurant serving lunch and dinner for $5 a plate. Pitchers of beer are $10 with three varieties. Projections are for revenue of $18,000 with a $9,000 profit. This new operating structure increases foot traffic and boat traffic to the marina increasing boat related sales of fuel and repair services by $14,000 each season. More traffic, more sales, more revenue.

At purchase, and just running the business "as bought" rental revenue was $100,000. Engaging in the business, changing the structure of the leases and adding land-based services increased revenue from $100,000 to:

Long-term leases: $80,000

Short-term leases: $38,000

Food Sales: $20,000

Services: $14,000

Total Revenue: $152,000

This is the same business, but with a new paradigm for use with RRT. The change going forward is in inserting the probability of short-term leases to increase revenue. Looking at just lease revenue, the change from single long-term leases to a mix of short-term and long-term increases Gross Potential Rent from $100,000 to $118,000 each year- an 18% single-year increase. The owners may find that a leasing mix with a higher percentage of short-term has greater potential to positively affect revenue. Testing, marketing application of good management should guide future changes.

Simplified:

RRT (%) = ((CR / GPR)(LT/12])/12) X 100)

With the following example, this shortened form is as follows:

Gross Potential Rent: GPR = $118,000

Collected Rents: CR = $115,758
                        (assumes no change in collections %)

Lease Term: LT = 12 months'

RRT (%) = (($115,758/$118,000)((12 - [12-12])/12) X 100)

= .9810%

= 98.10%

Property Type: Condominiums with Retail on Main Level

Case Background Information:

This property is becoming the norm in the heart of transportation districts in modern urban cities around the country such as Denver, Minneapolis, Seattle and Portland. Transportation districts provide large aspects of "livable cities" with a concentration of services (retail, restaurants, office and medical) directly connected to modes of transport that offer access to the larger metro.

Premise:

Polaris Condominium Association is on the pulse of everything the urbanite wants in a 24-hour city. A newer property with 54 one and two-bedroom condominium's, the project sold out before the last permit for construction issued. There is 8,300 square feet of retail leased at $13 per square foot with annually renewable leases. All store fronts are at street level with consistent pedestrian traffic.

The Association is responsible for paying taxes and insurance for the owners. The Association is also responsible for leasing the main level retail space. Board members (and owners) are feeling stress from continued increases in their real estate tax assessment- they keep going up at an exponential rate. They have hired counsel to try and slow the rate of increases to no avail. The only option seems to be to raise association fees yet again to keep pace.

The sole source of income outside of association fees is lease rents from the main level retail. Board members rotate the responsibilities of showing available space and try to select tenants that owners want to have in the building. According to "everybody" on the board lease rents are $13 a square foot for retail space in the area.

RRT Inputs:

    Gross Rent Potential = $120,848

    Stated Lease Rents = $107,900

    Collected Rents   = $102,505

    Lease Term = 1 year

Solve for RRT:

RRT (%) = A. $(107,900 \div 120,848 \times 100) = .8928\%$

        B. $(102,505 \div 107,900 \times 100) = .9500\%$

        C. $(1 - [12 - 12] \div 12) \times 100) = 100.00\%$

    = $(.8928\%)(.9500\%)(100\%)$

    = $.8448\%$

RRT Output: 84.48%

Simplified:

RRT (%) = ((CR / GPR)(LT/12])/12) X 100)

With the following example, this shortened form is as follows:

    Gross Potential Rent: GPR = $120,848

    Collected Rents: CR = $102,505

    Lease Term: LT = 12 months'

RRT (%) = (($102,505/$120,848)((12 - [12-12])/12) X 100)

    = 84.82%

When the only Board Members are home owners that's an easy red flag to spot. Most associations of any size hire professional association management companies. If this board were to hire an association management company their first order of business is probably to out-source leasing of the retail space to commercial brokers that do that for a living.

These "firewalls" (association management and commercial brokers) are working as service providers with the intention of maximizing revenue. Hiring professionals reduces the potential for nepotism and removes or diminishes the ability of a single strong board member from maintaining the status quo without merit (like retaining a lease to family member or keeping a coffee shop lease low just because they like the coffee).

To prove the point, presume the commercial broker market survey states lease rents are $18 today. How much money are they leaving on the table that could be coming in as an off-set to higher real estate taxes?

Simplified (Re-assessment):

RRT (%) = ((CR / GPR)(LT/12])/12) X 100)

With the following example, this shortened form is as follows:

Gross Potential Rent: GPR = $149,400

Collected Rents: CR = $102,505

Lease Term: LT = 12 months'

RRT (%) = (($102,505/$149,400)((12 - [12-12])/12) X 100)

= .6861%

= 68.61%

Solutions and Recommendations:
The answer is $46,895. The premise of the re-assessment is that GPR has moved from $120,858 to $149,400 with professional management identifying real time market rents (lease rents moving from $13.00 to $18.00. No waiting: bring in the commercial leasing professionals. Of course, this doesn't occur over-night. It may take a year or longer for pricing power to be in the hands of the new retail manager and their team. This is a simplified case study so please input a number for retaining leasing professionals, et al. What impact does this have for the homeowners? With an additional $46,895 per year in revenue, for the 54 homeowners this means that individual assessments may decrease by $868 each.

RRT ask a simple question: is GPR real? Are market rents, as suggested by the Board a reflection of market realities? In this case the answer was no- they were off by 27%. This is a representation of the importance of the numbers over a mere percent depiction: what is important is the change in real dollars from an assessment of GPR.

Property Type: Four-Story Urban Walk-up

Case Background Information:

The assets are in "downtown" Big City America. There is no parking, heavy pedestrian traffic and forty-four restaurants that deliver to your door 24/7. The building pre-dates WWII with multiple upgrades to assure operational integrity. It is a safe building and has a ferociously loyal resident base. Too bad there is no elevator- the value might double! Each story of the building is 6,300 square feet.

Premise:

The owner wonders out loud one day: "I wonder if we could put an elevator in". The old man has obviously gone crazy, but, he sends out his minions to check on feasibility. What comes back is "of course it's cost-prohibitive to install an elevator… however. (It's like when my wife says 'I've been thinking' – I love her to tears but I know that saying probably means trouble for me).

The "however" returns with options that may increase income. It will be a long process and a grueling couple of years- but there is the high probability that the main level could be re-zoned for retail/restaurant. Even better, if that were to occur, then, it is possible the second floor could be leased as office. Things that make your hmmmm. Things that make you thing – $$$~! Current income is $50,400 monthly.

AS OPERATED:

RRT Inputs:

     Gross Rent Potential = $622,944

     Stated Lease Rents = $604,800

     Collected Rents = $583,632

     Lease Term = 1 year

Solve for RRT:

RRT (%) = A. (604,800 ÷ 622,944 X 100) = .9708%

B. (583,632 ÷ 604,800 X 100) = .9649%

C. (1 – [12 – 12] ÷ 12) X 100) = 100.00 %

= (.9708%)(.9649%)(100%)

= .9367%

RRT Output: 93.67%

Simplified:

RRT (%) = ((CR / GPR)(LT/12])/12) X 100)

With the following example, this shortened form is as follows:

Gross Potential Rent: GPR = $622,944

Collected Rents: CR = $583,632
(assumes no change in collections %)

Lease Term: LT = 12 months'

RRT (%) = (($583,632/$622,944)((12 - [12-12])/12) X 100)

= .9368%

= 93.68%

AS CONVERTED TO RETAIL AND OFFICE ON TWO LEVELS:

The finished footprint on the main level is projected to have 5,000 square feet of leasable space considering city required build-outs. This space should lease for $35 per square foot annually, or GPR of $150,000. Office space, on the second level, is projected to have 6,000 square feet of rentable space at a price point of $22 per square foot, or $90,000. Because of the high demand ownership projects the same or higher rents for the remaining residential on floors 3 and 4 at $30,200 per month revenue. New revenue at conclusion of construction and lease up:

Residential - $362,400
Retail - $175,000
Office - $132,000
Total - $669,400

RRT Inputs:

Gross Rent Potential = $669,400

Stated Lease Rents = $641,326

Collected Rents = $615,672

Lease Term = 1 year

Solve for RRT:

RRT (%) = A. (641,326 ÷ 669,400 X 100) = .9580%

B. (615,672 ÷ 641,326 X 100) = .9599%

C. (1 − [12 − 12] ÷ 12) X 100) = 100.00%

= (.9580%)(.9599%)(100%)

= .9195%

RRT Output: 91.95%

Simplified:

RRT (%) = ((CR / GPR)(LT/12])/12) X 100)

With the following example, this shortened form is as follows:

Gross Potential Rent: GPR = $669,400

Collected Rents: CR = $615,672
                           (assumes no change in collections %)
Lease Term: LT = 12 months'

RRT (%) = (($615,672/$669,400)((12 - [12-12])/12) X 100)

= .9197%

= 91.97%

<u>Solutions and Recommendations:</u>

The probable increase in revenue is 5-7% and RRT decreases, meaning greater potential loss to lease likely from having varied uses in a single building. Will a neighborhood up-rising squash the whole thing after $500,000 in soft costs spent? Will the mayor attempt to make an example out of the zoning request as bad for the city because of reducing residential housing? Then consider the economic factors: will commercial rents remain at current levels, increase or decrease from projections? There is an exorbitant amount of risk with little upside potential. The old man should go back to playing golf and leave well enough alone...

The following case is blank on purpose for you to print and fill in the numbers.

Property Type: BLANK CASE

<u>Case Background Information:</u>

<u>Premise:</u>

RRT Inputs:

      Gross Rent Potential $_____

      Stated Lease Rents $_____

      Collected Rents $_____

      Lease Term _____

Solve for RRT:

RRT (%) = A. (_____ ÷ _____ X 100) = _____ %

           B. (_____ ÷ _____ X 100) = _____ %

           C. (1 – [12 – _____] ÷ 12) X 100) = _____ %

           = (_____ %)(._____ %)(_____ %)

           = ._____ %

RRT Output: _____ %

<u>Solutions and Recommendations:</u>

Simplified:

RRT (%) = ((CR / GPR)(LT/12])/12) X 100)

With the following example, this shortened form is as follows:

      Gross Potential Rent: GPR = $_____

      Collected Rents: CR = $_____

      Lease Term: LT = _____months'

RRT (%) = (($_____/$_____)((12 - [12-_____])/12) X 100)

      = ._____ %

      = _____ %

Conclusion

Rental property ownership is a business in constant motion as there are no two properties alike each having unique characteristics. Using the formula herein you have one more method to create some uniformity within your acquisitions process and increase the comfort level in the decisions made knowing that sometimes the best decision is to walk away. Better still, by going the extra mile, you will find viable opportunities lost on others because of their inability or unwillingness to look not only at the numbers, but behind, on top and underneath the numbers in a search for value.

The outputs from RRT represent an insightful perspective about the current operations of an asset operated as a rental property. As denoted earlier in the book, the money at stake is probably yours, so you have a sincere interest in making sure that a purchased asset fits within the risk parameters outlined by your investment criteria.

The ways investors measure risk varies. Most methods determine yield by a timeline that includes return of capital and a return on capital. RRT allows you to measure based on strength of income as represented in a single number allowing for a comparison amongst and between property that produce rental revenue. With confidence, you can compare a rental property asset with other similar assets and quickly separate those with promise.

The thinking behind this book is to provide you with a functional tool for the rental property buyer to get ahead of the process once the due diligence clock starts ticking. Further, I hope you will apply the metrics learned to better understand owned assets for purposes of unlocking value.

Thank you for taking this journey with me into evidence-based due diligence of rental property revenue using the Rent Roll Triangle formula as presented through these pages including the case studies.

Join me at JohnWilhoit.com for updates, blogs, books and podcast.

Please stay in touch. Look for my articles at Multifamily Insight.

Index

A

Acquisitions 1, 4
Apartments 86, 136, 142
Appreciation 6, 22

B

Budget 5, 30, 37, 47, 58, 62

C

Capital Expenditure 55, 61, 70
Census 83, 93, 95, 96
CMBS 12, 112, 150
Concessions 34, 45, 48
Construction Starts 82

D

Demographics 95, 96
Depreciation 7, 14, 18, 19, 23
Due Diligence 10, 16, 17, 27, 81, 97, 151

E

economy 28, 68, 106, 123, 140
Exit Strategy 18, 19, 20

F

Fannie Mae 151
Finance 111, 116, 127
Flooring 50, 51, 61, 132
Freddie Mac 151

G

Gartman 127
GDP 6, 122, 123, 124
Gross Domestic Product 106, 122, 123

H

Home Ownership 84, 137

www.ingramcontent.com/pod-product-compliance
Lightning Source LLC
Chambersburg PA
CBHW071454200326
41519CB00019B/5729